best hikes with
with
dogs
BOSTON & BEYOND

best hikes with dogs

BOSTON & BEYOND

Jenna Ringelheim

THE MOUNTAINEERS BOOKS

THE MOUNTAINEERS BOOKS
*is the nonprofit publishing arm of The Mountaineers Club, an organization
founded in 1906 and dedicated to the exploration, preservation, and
enjoyment of outdoor and wilderness areas.*

1001 SW Klickitat Way, Suite 201, Seattle, WA 98134

Copy Editor: Heath Silberfeld / enough said
Cover, Layout, and Book Design: The Mountaineers Books
Cartographer: Moore Creative Design
All photographs by the author unless otherwise noted.

Cover photograph: *Tasman soaks up the sun at the Middlesex
Fells Reservation.*
Frontispiece: *Ravenswood Park's trails are easy on the paws.*

Maps shown in this book were produced using National
Geographic's TOPO! software. For more information, go to
www.nationalgeographic.com/topo.

Library of Congress Cataloging-in-Publication Data
Ringelheim, Jenna.
  Best hikes with dogs : Boston and beyond / Jenna Ringelheim.—1st ed.
    p. cm.
  Includes index.
  ISBN 978-1-59485-052-3 (pbp)
  1. Hiking with dogs—Massachusetts—Boston Region—Guidebooks.
  2. Trails—Massachusetts—Boston Region—Guidebooks. 3. Boston Region
(Mass.)—Guidebooks. I. Title.
  SF427.455.R56 2008
  796.510974461—dc22
                              2008008068

This book is dedicated to Cobi, my first faithful companion and partner on the trail.

To a dog, motoring isn't just a way of getting from here to there, it's also a thrill and an adventure. The mere jingle of car keys is enough to send most any dog into a whimpering, tail-wagging frenzy.
—Jon Winokur

*Southfield's Mr. Pinks, aka Cobi,
1996–2005*

CONTENTS

Part 1: Hiking with Your Dog

Part 2: The Trails

North of Boston

Opposite: Tasman takes a break at the top of Maugus Hill.

Exploring Sea and Sand: The Cape and the Islands

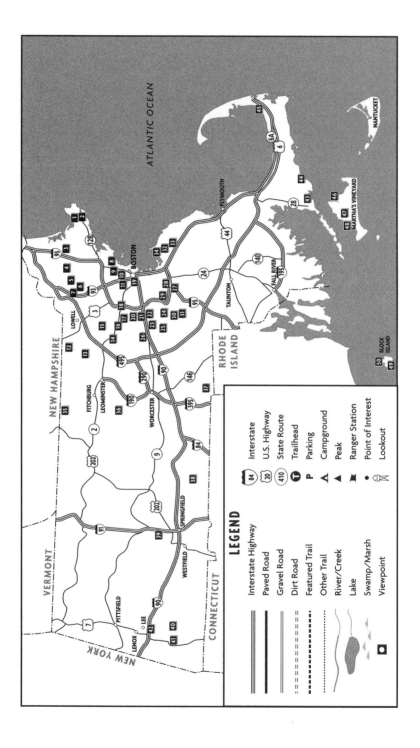

LEGEND

Interstate Highway	
Paved Road	
Gravel Road	
Dirt Road	
Featured Trail	
Other Trail	
River/Creek	
Lake	
Swamp/Marsh	
Viewpoint	

84	Interstate
20	U.S. Highway
410	State Route
T	Trailhead
P	Parking
▲	Campground
◀	Peak
▮	Ranger Station
•	Point of Interest
⌖	Lookout

HIKE SUMMARY TABLE

HIKE	3 miles or less	Easy on paws	Water feature	Off-leash opportunities	Scenic overlooks	Good for senior dogs	For active dogs only
North of Boston							
1. Dogtown Commons	●			●	●		
2. Ravenswood Park	●			●	●		
3. Appleton Farms Grass Rides	●	●		●		●	
4. Bald Hill Reservation				●			
5. Weir Hill Reservation	●	●	●	●			
6. Deer Jump Reservation			●	●	●	●	
7. Ward Reservation				●		●	
8. Lynn Woods	●	●					
9. Breakheart Reservation	●			●	●	●	●
10. Middlesex Fells Reservation: East Side	●			●		●	●
11. Middlesex Fells Reservation: West Side	●					●	
Northwest of Boston							
12. Dunstable Rural Land Trust Wildlife Preserve	●	●	●	●		●	
13. Groton Place and Sabine Woods	●	●	●	●		●	
14. Spring Hill/Nashoba Brook Conservation Areas				●	●		
15. Great Brook Farm State Park	●	●	●	●		●	
16. Estabrook Woods/Punkatasset Conservation Land	●			●	●		
17. Lincoln Conservation Land/Mount Misery	●	●	●	●		●	
18. Willards Woods	●	●	●	●		●	
West of Boston							
19. Fresh Pond Reservation	●	●	●	●	●	●	
20. Cat Rock Park	●	●	●	●	●		
21. Weston Reservoir	●	●	●	●		●	
22. Centennial Reservation	●	●	●	●	●		
23. Elm Bank Reservation	●	●	●	●		●	
24. Noanet Woodlands				●	●	●	●
25. Rocky Narrows/Sherborn Town Forest	●			●	●	●	●
26. Callahan State Park/Welch Reservation	●			●	●		

HIKE	3 miles or less	Easy on paws	Water feature	Off-leash opportunities	Scenic overlooks	Good for senior dogs	For active dogs only
South of Boston							
27. Blue Hills Reservation: Great Blue Hill	•				•		•
28. Blue Hills Reservation: Ponkapoag Pond		•	•			•	
29. Wilson Mountain Reservation	•		•				
30. Rocky Woods			•	•	•		•
31. Noon Hill	•		•	•	•		•
32. Whitney and Thayer Woods	•			•			
33. Wompatuck State Park				•			•
34. Worlds End Reservation		•	•		•		
Doggie Daytrip: Central/Western Massachusetts							
35. Mount Watatic			•	•	•		•
36. Wachusett Mountain State Reservation	•				•		•
37. Douglas State Forest	•		•				
38. Peaked Mountain	•		•	•	•		•
39. Mount Tom State Reservation	•		•		•		•
40. Beartown State Forest	•	•	•			•	
41. Monument Mountain	•		•		•		•
42. October Mountain State Forest		•	•			•	
Exploring Sea and Sand: The Cape and the Islands							
43. Beebe Woods	•	•	•			•	
44. Mashpee River Woodlands			•		•	•	
45. Nickerson State Park			•			•	
46. Trade Wind Fields Preserve	•	•	•	•		•	
47. Waskosims Rock Reservation	•				•	•	
48. Great Rock Bight Preserve	•			•	•	•	
49. Rodmans Hollow	•			•	•	•	
50. Clay Head Preserve		•	•	•	•	•	

AUTHOR'S NOTE

While taking a hike on a wonderful spring afternoon, my first Portuguese water dog passed away. Cobi had been diagnosed the previous fall with lymphoma of the eye, and the tumor ultimately had spread, causing his heart to stop on that day in 2005. After an emotional good-bye at the Tufts Veterinary Hospital, I returned home to find a heart-wrenching email in my inbox: a request for a proposal from The Mountaineers Books for a book that was to be entitled *Best Hikes with Dogs: Boston and Beyond*.

The story of how I was able to write this book began long before that day. For as long as I can remember, I have loved dogs and, more important, hiking with dogs. Before Cobi arrived in my family's life I would often borrow Chessie, the shaggy shepherd mix that lived down the street, for afternoon jaunts in the local woods. When I went to college, Cobi came along, and we explored the Adirondacks together. Later, when I moved to Idaho and Oregon, Cobi learned (and loved) to go on backpacking trips in the Sawtooth Mountains and along the Oregon coast. Cobi and I were partners on the trails.

After returning to the East Coast for graduate school, I was initially discouraged with the outdoor opportunities for people and their pets. Signs that read "No Dogs Allowed" or "Leashes Required" littered the local open spaces. Upon further investigation, though, I discovered new areas to explore and over time became pleasantly surprised to find some great hikes that were close to the city—and that allowed Cobi to romp leash free.

When I was offered the opportunity to write this book, the one caveat was that I had to get another dog. That decision was an easy one, and in the fall of 2005 a second Portuguese water dog entered my life. Tasman, being the lucky dog that he is, spent the first couple years of his life hiking more than seventy trails in Massachusetts and Rhode Island.

Writing this book has been a labor of love, not only for the amazing places that I have been able to investigate but also for the two dogs that have taught me so much along the way. My hope is that you and your four-legged companions enjoy the trails as much as we have.

ACKNOWLEDGMENTS

First and foremost, I want to thank my family for being so supportive during the two years that it took to complete this endeavor: my sister, Kayla, for her amazing organizational skills—I may never have finished without her; my mom, Cyndi, my great hiking partner and person to bounce ideas off; Steve, the camera guru, who let me borrow his digital camera until I bought one of my own; and my brother, Matt, who always would ask "Are you done yet?"

Second, I must thank the family and friends who accompanied me on the trails: thank you, Joan, for joining me on my first and last hikes; and thanks to Lauren B., who was always willing to explore another new place; to Teddy and Robi, who helped me investigate the Berkshires; and to Tom, for taking a whirlwind tour of Block Island. Thanks to the Levys for sharing their lovely house, so I could spend some time on Cape Cod. Thanks are also due to Lauren W., Liz, Becky, Ryan, Sam, Josh, Meghan, Lynda, Eva, Amy, Alex, Joyce, and Barbara.

To Tasman's friends—Greta, Abby, Mac, Olive, Simba, Paco, Willy, Dylan, Solomon, Razzie, Shadow, Lani, and Kai—who sniffed, swam, scrambled, frolicked, drooled, played, and, most of all, hiked along all these trails.

Thanks to the staff at The Mountaineers Books for having faith in a first-time author and providing not only an amazing opportunity but also guiding me along the way. And to Heath Silberfeld, who edited this book with a tremendous amount of patience and attention to detail.

Most important, I want to acknowledge all the lovely people and pets I met on the trails who shared their favorite places to play outdoors. It is because of them that this book highlights the best hikes with dogs, Boston and beyond!

PART 1

Hiking with Your Dog

Heading out on a hike with your friends takes preparation, but heading out with your furry friend takes preparation to a whole other level. Nothing is better than taking a hike with your dog. Being prepared for the trail not only makes the experience more enjoyable for you and your pup—it also will ensure that dog-friendly places remain that way for years to come.

Good Dogs Require Good Owners

Someone once told me that there was no such thing as a bad dog—just dogs with bad owners. Good dogs need training, and training should begin the minute your cute little ball of fur enters your home. Now, I'm not saying that your dog should know how to roll over on the second day—dog ownership is like any other friendship: the relationship of trust builds over time.

The best place to start is with a basic obedience class. Trainers can be found through your vet or at the local pet store, but you can't just sign

Dylan waits patiently on the ferry to Martha's Vineyard. (Photo by Steve Birnbaum)

up for a class and expect that your dog is going to be perfect at the end of eight sessions. Training is a journey, not a destination. Even your elderly dog can be reminded to heel, sit, and stay.

Socialization is another important part of good dog ownership. Dogs that travel the trails need to be comfortable with other dogs—and people. When your pup is young, schedule playdates with other doggie friends. Walk your dog around town regularly until he or she is comfortable with people of all shapes and sizes.

Once your dog is old enough to learn basic commands, a plethora of words come in handy on the trail:

Sit: This one is pretty self-explanatory.

Stay: Don't move, I'll be right back.

Come: You are too far ahead on the trail. Get back here!

Wait: Hold on a second until I tell you it is safe.

Leave it: I promise, that horse manure really isn't that good.

Shake: You are really wet. Would you mind drying off, please?

Over: You need to jump over this log, okay?

Water: Find the lake. It's time for a swim!

Quiet: Everyone in the campground is sleeping. Shhh!

Load up: Play time is over. It's time to get in the car.

If you hope to have a well-behaved off-leash dog, start training early and train often. Dogs that are used to coming on command regularly are usually better at it. If running off leash is only a special treat, exciting distractions can frequently override the command. Creating a unique recall whistle is helpful when encountering other dogs and their owners.

To Leash or Not to Leash: That Is the Question

Every dog is different, and some are better able than others to behave off leash while hiking. Rules and regulations change regularly in regard to dogs, so even if your dog can walk without a leash it is important to always have one available.

Educating yourself about where you can take your dog during different times of the year is also important. For example, many of the beaches in Massachusetts allow dogs, but hours are restricted in summer. Some properties allow your dog to roam leash free—but only after you are a certain distance away from the trailhead. Other places allow dogs to be off leash if they are licensed in that particular town or if they retain a special permit. (See "The Trustees of Reservations Green Dogs Program.")

If you are concerned about the pet policies at a particular place, call ahead to the appropriate land manager. Most important, however, is that you must know your own dog. If potential hazards are going to be way too tempting for your pooch to ignore, using a leash is always a good option.

The Trustees of Reservations Green Dogs Program

In April 2002, the Trustees began an innovative pilot dog-walking program to ensure that all visitors are able to enjoy Trustees properties and have access to an environment that is safe, comfortable, and healthy for dogs, dog owners, and all other visitors. The program is currently in place at Rocky Woods and Appleton Farms.

The Green Dogs Program regulations can be found in more detail by doing a search on The Trustees of Reservations website (www.ttor.org) or by calling (508) 785-0339. Enrollment in the Green Dogs program is handled at the Rocky Woods main entrance only (see Hike 30 for directions). To be eligible for a permit, bring your Trustees of Reservations membership card. If you're not a member yet, you can join at the same time you register for the permit by bringing each dog you are enrolling and each dog's up-to-date town dog license.

Canine Trail Etiquette

It only takes one irresponsible dog owner to ruin it for everyone else who likes to hike with dogs. With more people (and dogs) on the trails every year, appropriate access for dogs to parks and open spaces has become a hotly debated issue. For those who wish to see these "best hikes with dogs" remain that way, it is important to make note of the following "Ten Canons of Canine Trail Etiquette":

1. Keep the dog-to-human ratio at 1:1.
2. Limit the total number of dogs in your hiking group to three, regardless of the number of humans.
3. Put your dog on a leash whenever you meet others—people or dogs—on the trail.
4. Hikers without dogs have the right-of-way.
5. No jumping up, sniffing, licking, growling, or barking allowed.
6. Shout a friendly hello to tell your dog when a friend, not a foe, approaches.

7. Clean up after your dog—that includes dog poop.
8. Obey the rules of the trail.
9. Stay on the trail.
10. Leave plants and wild animals alone.

Happy, Healthy Trails

Some people like to run marathons, and others enjoy an evening stroll around the block. Dogs are the same way—each has an individual level of fitness. Just because you are a weekend warrior does not mean that your mostly sedentary dog is going to enjoy a full day of hiking. Like obedience, a regular exercise regime is very important for your dog.

When training for the trails, start simple. A walk in the morning and evening is a good place to begin. If your dog is ready for more, try a short run. All these activities will help with your dog's endurance and, more important, will toughen tender pads. Remember, though, that it

Dogs of all sizes are good hiking companions.

is important not to overdo training. Growing puppies should not start hiking until they are at least one year old since uneven terrain and repetitive motion can do permanent damage to their developing hips, shoulders, and other joints. It is just as important to take it easy with older dogs that might have arthritis, stiff joints, or other ailments.

Choosing a breed that matches your level of activity is essential. An English bulldog might look incredibly cute curled up on your couch but might not want to climb a mountain with you. That being said, a trail definitely exists for every kind of dog, so choose your trails wisely and everyone should have a good time.

A quick vet checkup before the first big outing is also essential. Make sure that your dog has all the necessary shots, particularly rabies. You never know what kind of animal you and your pooch might run into in the woods. Also, some state parks require proof of vaccination and an up-to-date rabies tag. Ask your vet about any other prevalent mosquito- or water-borne diseases in your area. Lyme disease is found throughout Massachusetts and Rhode Island, so you might consider using a topical tick deterrent, which your vet can provide.

Your first few outings should be short day hikes. These will allow your dog to learn the rules of the trail, while experiencing all the new sights, smells, and sounds. If your dog takes to longer-distance hiking, you might want to invest in a pair of dog booties, which come in handy on rocky terrain, where there might be broken glass, or as an extra layer of protection if your dog injures a pad. Gear for your dog is covered in more detail in "The Top Ten Canine Essentials" section.

Leave No Trace

When hiking the trails of Massachusetts and Rhode Island (or any place for that matter), the Leave No Trace Principles of outdoor ethics are paramount (see www.LNT.org):

1. Plan ahead and prepare.
2. Travel and camp on durable surfaces.
3. Dispose of waste properly.
4. Leave what you find.
5. Minimize campfire impacts.
6. Respect wildlife.
7. Be considerate of other visitors.

Opposite: Spring hikes offer the beauty of wildflowers in bloom.

Plan Ahead and Prepare

- Know the regulations and special concerns for the area you'll visit.
- Prepare for extreme weather, hazards, and emergencies.
- Schedule your trip to avoid times of high use.
- Visit in small groups. Split larger parties into groups of four to six.
- Repackage food to minimize waste.
- Use a map and compass to eliminate the use of marking paint, rock cairns, or flagging.

Travel and Camp on Durable Surfaces

- Durable surfaces include established trails and campsites, rock, gravel, dry grasses, or snow.
- Protect riparian areas by camping at least 200 feet from lakes and streams.
- Good campsites are found, not made. Altering a site is not necessary.
- In popular areas:
  Concentrate use on existing trails and campsites.
  Walk single file in the middle of the trail, even when it's wet or muddy.
  Keep campsites small. Focus activity in areas where vegetation is absent.
- In pristine areas:
  Disperse use to prevent the creation of campsites and trails.
  Avoid places where impacts are just beginning.

Dispose of Waste Properly

- Pack it in, pack it out. Inspect your campsite and rest areas for trash or spilled foods. Pack out all trash, leftover food, and litter.
- Deposit solid human waste in catholes dug 6 to 8 inches deep at least 200 feet from water, camp, and trails. Cover and disguise the cathole when finished.
- Pack out toilet paper and hygiene products.
- To wash yourself or your dishes, carry water 200 feet away from streams or lakes and use small amounts of biodegradable soap. Scatter strained dishwater.

Gnawed trees are a sign of beaver activity.

Leave What You Find

- Preserve the past: examine, but do not touch, cultural or historic structures and artifacts.
- Leave rocks, plants, and other natural objects as you find them.
- Avoid introducing or transporting nonnative species.
- Do not build structures or furniture; do not dig trenches.

Minimize Campfire Impacts

- Campfires can cause lasting impacts to the backcountry. Use a lightweight stove for cooking and enjoy a candle lantern for light.
- Where fires are permitted, use established fire rings, fire pans, or mound fires.
- Keep fires small. Only use sticks from the ground that can be broken by hand.
- Burn all wood and coals to ash, put out campfires completely, then scatter cool ashes.

Respect Wildlife

- Observe wildlife from a distance. Do not follow or approach any wildlife.
- Never feed animals. Doing so damages wildlife health, alters natural behaviors, and exposes wildlife to predators and other dangers.
- Protect wildlife and your food by storing rations and trash securely.
- Control pets at all times, or leave them at home.
- Avoid wildlife during sensitive times: in winter, or when mating, nesting, or raising young.

Be Considerate of Other Visitors

- Respect other visitors and protect the quality of their experience.
- Be courteous. Yield to other users on the trail.
- Step to the downhill side of the trail when encountering pack stock.
- Take breaks and camp away from trails and other visitors.
- Let nature's sounds prevail. Avoid loud voices and noises.

Getting into Gear

Whether you plan to be gone for a week or just an afternoon, packing appropriately for the outdoors is essential. My motto is "Be prepared for the worst—but expect only the best." Simple things, such as wearing synthetic materials rather than cotton or packing light raingear and an extra pair of socks, will make you much more comfortable on the trail. To take proper care of your pet along the trail, you have to be prepared to care for yourself.

The Ten Essentials

The Mountaineers' Ten Essentials are important recommendations to adhere to when hiking in Massachusetts and Rhode Island. Make note: This is not a comprehensive list for a weeklong backpack but rather a checklist of the basics needed when hitting the trails.

1. Navigation (map and compass)
2. Sun protection (sunglasses and sunscreen)
3. Insulation (extra clothing)
4. Illumination (headlamp or flashlight)

5. First-aid supplies
6. Fire (firestarter and matches/lighter)
7. Repair kit and tools (including knife)
8. Nutrition (extra food)
9. Hydration (extra water)
10. Emergency shelter

The Top Five People Essentials

I have my own top five essentials for people, which overlap with The Mountaineers' Ten Essentials:

1. **Extra food and clothing:** Weather in New England can change quickly, so it is important to be prepared for any conditions. Even on a short hike, bring some energy bars and plenty of water for you and your dog. A lightweight raincoat and an extra layer for warmth often come in handy.
2. **Sun protection:** Invest in a good pair of sunglasses, and bring sunscreen with an SPF no less than 30. A hat and a lightweight button-down shirt can also protect you from the sun.
3. **Basic first aid:** Buy a prepackaged kit or make your own. Bandages, antiseptic, and aspirin are essential. Bring duct tape for those times when everything else fails to meet your needs.
4. **Orienteering tools:** The techno wiz may want to bring a Global Positioning System (GPS), while others may prefer a map and compass. Whatever you choose, find something that works for you as you navigate the trails.
5. **Emergency firestarter and illumination:** Nothing is worse than being cold and in the dark. Matches or a lighter are great when you need to start a fire. A headlamp is invaluable when you are heading back to the trailhead after dark.

The Top Ten Canine Essentials

Let's face it: getting new gear for the trail is fun. Just as you might appreciate the importance of a good pair of hiking boots, your dog will be much happier if he is outfitted with the appropriate accessories. Many companies make gear specifically for dogs on the trail, including backpacks, booties, and packable feeding bowls. Unless you are planning on sharing your sleeping bag with your furry friend, make sure you bring a fleece blanket or piece of thermal pad for your dog to sleep on for overnights.

The following are the ten essentials I recommend for your dog:

1. **Obedience training:** Before you set foot on a trail, make sure your dog is trained and can be trusted to behave when faced with other hikers, other dogs, wildlife, and the vast assortment of unfamiliar scents and sights found in the outdoors.

2. **Doggy backpack:** Let your dog carry its own gear, but make sure that the load is appropriate to your dog's weight and size.

3. **Basic first-aid kit:** (See "What Goes in a Canine First-Aid Kit?")

4. **Dog food and trail treats:** Bring more food than your dog normally consumes since he will be burning more calories than normal, and if you do end up spending an extra night out, you need to keep your pup fed, too. Trail treats serve the same purpose for dogs as they do for you—quick energy and a pick-me-up during a strenuous day of hiking.

5. **Water and water bowl:** Don't count on finding water along the trail for your dog. Pack enough extra water to meet all of your dog's drinking needs.

6. **Leash and collar, or harness:** Even if your dog is fully trained to voice commands and can heel without a leash, sometimes leashes are required by law, or need to be used as a common courtesy, so have one handy at all times. A harness provides additional control when traveling along trickier parts of the trail.

7. **Insect repellent:** I prefer DEET-free bug repellents, many of which are citronella based and gentler on the skin. If you decide to use a DEET-based repellent, be aware that some animals, and some people, have strong negative reactions to them. Long before you head out to hike, dab a little DEET-based repellent on a patch of your dog's fur to watch for a reaction. Look for signs of drowsiness, lethargy, or nausea. Restrict repellent applications to those places the dog can't lick, staying clear of the ears and inner ears. The back of the neck and around the ears are the places mosquitoes most likely will be looking for exposed skin to bite.

8. **ID tags and picture identification:** Your dog should always wear ID tags. I heartily recommend microchipping, too, whereby a vet injects a tiny encoded microchip under the skin between a dog's shoulders. If your dog ever gets lost and is picked up by animal control, or is taken to a vet's office, a quick

A harness often comes in handy on the trail.

pass over the dog's back with a hand scanner will reveal the chip and allow the staff at that shelter or hospital to identify your dog and notify you. Microchipping is so prevalent that virtually every veterinarian and animal shelter automatically checks for chips by scanning unknown dogs they encounter. You should always carry a picture identification in your pack. If your dog gets lost, you can use the picture to show other hikers and to make flyers to post in the surrounding communities.

9. **Dog booties:** These can be used to protect your dog's feet from rough ground and harsh vegetation. They are also great for keeping bandages secure around damaged pads.

10. **Compact roll of plastic bags and trowel:** You'll use the plastic bags to clean up after your dog on popular trails. When conditions warrant, you can use the trowel to bury your dog's waste. Dig a small hole, deposit the dog waste, and fill in the hole, making sure the waste is covered by a few inches of soil.

Canine First Aid

Having a canine first-aid kit is necessary, even if it contains only the bare-bones essentials. Anyone heading into the wild with a canine companion for an extended trip should carry the following requisites for a complete, comprehensive, canine first-aid kit:

Instruments

Scissors/bandage scissors/toenail clippers
Rectal thermometer (a healthy dog should show a rectally obtained
temperature of 101°F)

Cleansers and disinfectants

3% hydrogen peroxide
Betadine
Canine eyewash (available at any large pet supply store or vet's
office)

Topical antibiotics and ointments (nonprescription)

Calamine lotion
Triple antibiotic ointment (bacitracin, neomycin, and polymyxin)
Baking soda (for stings)
Petroleum jelly
Stop-bleeding powder

Medications

Any prescription medications your dog needs
Enteric-coated aspirin or Bufferin
Imodium-AD
Pepto-Bismol

Dressings and bandages

Gauze pads (4 inches square) or gauze roll
Nonstick pads
Adhesive tape (1-inch and 2-inch rolls)

Miscellaneous

Muzzle
Dog booties

For Extended Trips

Consult your vet about any other prescription medications that may be needed in emergency situations, including the following:

Oral antibiotics

Eye/ear medications

Emetics (to induce vomiting)

Pain and anti-inflammatory medication

Suturing materials for large open wounds

Obstacles, Weather, and All Things Wild

My dog knows we are going hiking as soon as we turn onto a dirt road. Yet for dogs that are new to the outdoors, the peculiar things that surround them can sometimes become overwhelming. Even the most well-behaved dog can get in trouble on the trail. Knowing what might be ahead of you is half the battle.

Hunting Season

Many of the trails outlined in this book are within areas that permit hunting in season. Depending on the type of dog you have, a hunter might mistake the pooch for his next trophy. Invest in a brightly colored dog vest, and contact the land manager to find out when you should avoid the trails entirely.

Rocky Outcroppings and Overlooks

Even the most sure-footed dogs can lose their balance. On rocky trails, always have a leash available, and if you want a little more control, look into purchasing a harness.

Riptides, Floods, and Waterfalls

Knowing your dog's swimming ability will help you gauge where it is okay to go for a dip. Always use extra precaution at the beach, as riptides are often hard to detect from the shoreline. Although flash floods are not particularly common, rivers and streams can become quite the obstacles after a steady downpour. Even though waterfalls are beautiful, you should avoid them when hiking with your dog.

Heat

You might have the most free time in the heat of summer, but that is not

Greta soaks up the sun in the Middlesex Fells.

necessarily the best time of year to go hiking with your dog. Heatstroke is one of the most dangerous illnesses on the trail and can become a life-threatening condition. A dog's cooling system is extremely inefficient, as dogs sweat only through their footpads and tongue. Signs of heatstroke include excessive panting, increased heart rate, and pale gums. To avoid heatstroke, make sure your dog is hydrated and has plentiful access to shade along the trail. Also, hike in the early morning or evening to beat the heat.

Plants and Other Pests

Several plants and animals commonly encountered on trails in Massachusetts and Rhode Island can cause problems for dogs. Plants and animals of concern include the following:

Poison ivy. Although dogs are less susceptible to poison ivy due to the protection from their coat, that is not to say that they can't rub the itch-causing oils onto you. Keep an eye on the trail, and if you are concerned that the pooch or you has touched it, wash as soon as possible with soap and water.

Rhododendrons and azaleas. Known for their beautiful flowers, these bushes and their leaves can be toxic to dogs. Never use the branches for a game of fetch.

Grasses and seeds. Although these are more of an annoyance than an actual danger, steer clear of tall grassy areas to avoid burrs, thistle, and other sharp-edged plants that can get caught in your dog's fur and paws.

Ticks and mosquitoes. Ticks and mosquitoes can carry a variety of doggie diseases, including but not limited to Lyme disease, heartworm, and West Nile virus. Check with your vet for the most pertinent vaccinations, and be prepared with bug spray on the trail. Ticks range in size from a pinhead to a small pea. If you find one on your dog, don't worry as it can be easily removed. Take a pair of tweezers and grasp the tick at the head. Use a slow and steady motion to pull the head straight out of the skin. Once you are done, wash the area with soap and water.

Dogs can get Lyme disease from an infected tick that passes bacteria into the bloodstream when it bites. The tick must remain attached to the animal's skin for at least one day before the bacteria can be transmitted, so if you check your dog for ticks every day, you have a better chance of preventing the disease. Without treatment, Lyme disease can cause problems in many parts of your dog's body, including the heart, kidneys, and joints. On rare occasions, it can lead to neurological disorders. Symptoms can include high fever, swollen lymph nodes, lameness, and a loss of appetite. If you suspect that your dog might be sick, visit your vet, who can prescribe the appropriate medicine.

Horses, deer, and other hoofed animals. For dogs that spend most of their days in the city, the sight of a large equine, bovine,

Before hitting the trails, form a good relationship with your vet.

or ungulate can generate a variety of responses. Beyond getting kicked, another danger of running into one of these animals is that your dog may chase it and end up disoriented and far away from you. Socializing your dog to domesticated farm animals can help, but your dog's response to deer can be less predictable. Have a leash handy for times of need.

Although unlikely, you may also run into a stray moose in the woods. If a moose blocks the trail, yell loudly to scare it away. If it seems aggressive—drops it ears or looks agitated—take a detour with your leashed dog. If it charges, run. Moose are not predatory, so once the threat is no longer perceived, this gangly animal often will saunter away.

Poison ivy—leaves of three, let it be!

Porcupines, skunks, and raccoons. These three animals provide another good reason to keep your dog leashed while hiking in the backcountry. Nothing can ruin a hike faster than a face full of quills or the odorous spray of a skunk. If your dog encounters a porcupine, grab the quills near your pup's skin and give a quick assertive pull. Most dogs will tolerate only one or two painful yanks, so a follow-up visit to the vet and a sedative may be required. Many old wives' tales tell one how to remove the spray of a skunk, but sadly most of them do not work. The combination of wet dog and skunk spray is less than appealing, but over time (and many shampoos) the smell will dissipate. A rabid raccoon is another animal to avoid on the trail and remains a good reminder to always keep your dog's vaccinations up to date.

Bears. The black bear is the only species of bear still living in the Northeast. In Massachusetts, they are most commonly found in the wilder parts, such as the Berkshires and along the New Hampshire border. If you find yourself close to a bear, these guidelines may help you:

- Remain calm and talk in a low-pitched voice.
- Keep a firm grip on your dog's leash at a heeling length.
- Do not run, as this might trigger a prey-chase reaction.
- Do not look the bear in the eye. Bears perceive eye contact as a threat or a challenge.
- Move slowly away and upwind so the bear can smell that you are human.
- If a bear charges, stand your ground, as it may be a bluff. If it attacks, let go of your dog and fight back. This is a rare behavior for black bears, but it is possible. Once a black bear realizes that you are not easy prey, it might leave.

Choosing Trails for Dogs

This book is not meant to be a comprehensive guide to all hiking areas that allow dogs in Massachusetts and Rhode Island, but it does give a good sampling of dog-friendly places across these two states. Each trail was chosen for its unique qualities, with the bare necessities of shade, access to water, and flexible leash laws kept in mind. Many of the hikes offer opportunities to extend or shorten the distance or to access a nearby hike. Some hikes were picked for their proximity to the city, while others were included for their less-traveled trails. You will find a hike in this book for young dogs and old, as well as walks that are appropriate for

Solomon loves visiting Centennial Reservation.

dogs of all fitness levels. In general, a trail is a good choice for your dog if it has the following:

- Streams, lakes, ponds, or any other body of water in which your dog can take a dip
- Shade for much of the hike
- No major roads or vehicular traffic to cross
- No leash requirement (although a leash should be available at all times)
- No sharp rocks or broken glass
- A trailhead that is easily accessible by vehicle
- Other friendly dogs and owners along the trail

Alternative Transit in the City

Do you live in the city without a car and wish you could take your dog for a nice walk in the woods? Don't fret. You and your pooch can access the trails in this book in multiple ways.

Public Transit

Public transit in the Boston area is surprisingly pet friendly. Service animals are allowed on all forms of public transit at all times. The average pooch can travel by T, bus, train, and boat. Vehicle operators have a say in whether or not your dog may ride, so make sure yours is properly leashed, behaves politely, and stays off the seats. On trains and buses, dogs are allowed only during off-peak hours. Dogs are allowed on commuter boats at all hours of every day. For more information about peak and off-peak hours, schedules, and routes, visit www.mbta.com.

Zipcar

For hikes that are a bit farther away, Zipcar provides a great alternative to get you and your pooch to the trailhead. Zipcar is a membership-based car-sharing company that provides to its members automobile rentals that are billable by the hour or day. Each vehicle—from trucks to hybrids—has a home location: a reserved parking space located on a street, driveway, or neighborhood parking lot. Zipcars can be found all over the Boston metro area and in parts of western Massachusetts. Dogs are allowed in Zipcars but must be kept in pet carriers. Members are responsible for the removal of any pet hair. To learn more, check out www.zipcar.com.

How to Use This Book

The beginning of each hike description includes a summary of the most important hike details, including length, contact information, and rules for the trail.

Location is the municipality in which the particular hike can be found. Some natural areas highlighted in this book span multiple towns.

The hike's total mileage is given as **Distance**. Several hikes offer opportunities to lengthen or shorten the hike. If this is the case, additional information is given about the length of the different options.

Hiking time is an estimate, knowing that a Great Dane and a Chihuahua are likely to hike at different speeds. When hiking with dogs, you're likely to encounter many exciting distractions, including swimming holes and fun stuff to sniff, but a dog and owner will hike on average a thirty-minute mile. The total for more strenuous hikes includes some time to stop and enjoy the view.

Elevation gain is determined by calculating the difference between the highest and lowest points along the trail. If that difference is less than

100 feet, the elevation gain is considered negligible. An elevation profile is provided for gains over 100 feet.

Each hike has an associated **Map** (or Maps). The United States Geological Survey (USGS) maps can be found at local bookstores, outdoors stores, and online retailers. If a map has been made locally, contact information is provided.

The **Contact** for each hike is often the land manager from whom you can obtain updates on trail conditions or any new rules for dogs.

The **Pet policy** can change frequently, and although this book aims to give you the best and most updated information available, it never hurts to double-check before hitting the trails.

Some trails will have **Special notes** that may warn you about hunting seasons or other potential hazards along the trail.

Getting there provides driving directions to the trailhead from a major highway or the nearest town. If feasible, consider taking public transit to the trailhead.

Long-Distance and Regional Trails in Massachusetts

With active trail organizations and a history of conservation, Massachusetts is fortunate to have a variety of long-distance and regional trails.

Appalachian Trail

Distance: 90 miles in Massachusetts

Description: The Appalachian National Scenic Trail (AT) is a passive recreation footpath that runs 2175 miles from Springer Mountain in Georgia to Mount Katahdin in Maine. In Massachusetts, the trail runs along ridges and traverses the valleys of Berkshire County.

Website: www.appalachiantrail.org

Bay Circuit Trail

Distance: 150 miles

Description: When complete, this trail will be nearly 200 miles long, connecting parks and conservation land all the way around metropolitan Boston. Sections of the trail have been completed in Newbury, Ipswich, Topsfield, Middleton, Boxford, North Andover, and Andover.

Website: www.baycircuit.org

Samson and Tasman wait for a treat.

Metacomet–Monadnock Trail (M–M Trail)

Distance: 114 miles

Description: Maintained by the Appalachian Mountain Club–Berkshire Chapter Trails Committee and other volunteers, the M–M Trail passes through some of the prettiest landscape in western Massachusetts, including the Mount Tom State Reservation, Mount Holyoke Range and Skinner State Parks, and numerous other state, municipal, and land trust properties.

Website: www.amcberkshire.org/mm-trail

Midstate Trail

Distance: 92 miles

Description: From Mount Watatic in Ashburnham on the New Hampshire state line and south to Douglas State Forest on the Rhode Island state line, the Midstate Trail passes through Leominster, Wachusett Mountain, Rutland, and Douglas State Forest.

Website: www.midstatetrail.org

Tully Trail

Distance: 22 miles

Description: The Tully Trail travels from Tully Mountain north to Tully Lake, Doane's Falls, Jacob's Hill, and Royalston Falls, then south through the Warwick State Forest.

Website: www.thetrustees.org/pages/37_tully_trail.cfm

Wapack Trail

Distance: 21 miles

Description: This trail follows the northern end of the Midstate Trail at Mount Watatic in Ashburnham, Massachusetts, to Greenville, New Hampshire, with an additional 7 miles of side trails. The Wapack crosses the summits of Watatic, Pratt, New Ipswich, Barrett, and Temple Mountains, then ascends the South and North Pack Monadnocks and has many scenic vistas from open ledges.

Website: www.wapack.org

A Note About Safety

Safety is an important concern in all outdoor activities. No guidebook can alert you to every hazard or anticipate the limitations of every reader. Therefore, the descriptions of roads, trails, routes, and natural features in this book are not representations that a particular place or excursion will be safe for your party. When you follow any of the routes described in this book, you assume responsibility for your own safety. Under normal conditions, such excursions require the usual attention to traffic, road and trail conditions, weather, terrain, the capabilities of your party, and other factors. Because many of the lands in this book are subject to development and/or change of ownership, conditions may have changed since this book was written that make your use of some of these routes unwise. Always check for current conditions, obey posted private property signs, and avoid confrontations with property owners or managers. Keeping informed on current conditions and exercising common sense are the keys to a safe, enjoyable outing.

The Mountaineers Books

PART 2

The Trails

NORTH OF BOSTON

1. Dogtown Commons

Location: Gloucester
Distance: 2.5 miles round-trip
Hiking time: 1.5 hours
Elevation gain: Negligible
Map: USGS Rockport
Contact: The City of Gloucester, (978) 281-9781
Pet policy: Dogs are allowed leashed or under voice control.
Special notes: Hunting season is October 19 through April 1, Monday–Saturday. Wear bright colors, and proceed with caution. Adjacent to the Dogtown Commons entrance is the Cape Ann Sportsman's Club. If your dog spooks easily, leash up for the beginning of the hike.

Getting there: Take Route 128 toward Gloucester. From the Grant Circle Rotary, take the Route 127 north exit, and then turn right onto Reynard Street. Drive less than a mile, then turn left onto Cherry Street, continue for about a mile, and turn right onto Dogtown Road. Continue along the road until you reach a gate. Park on the right side of the road.

The name alone should spark enough interest for you and your pooch to check this place out. Once a farming community, Dogtown Commons represents one of the few deserted villages in New England. Settled in the early eighteenth century, it was abandoned by 1830, leaving only dogs to roam the area. Today, this open space is comprised of 3000 acres of fields, forest, reservoirs, and marshes, with so much terrain that you and your pup will keep coming back for more. Most of Dogtown is dense woodland,

Tasman and Paco take a break at a Babson boulder.

crisscrossed and bisected by trails and old roads that make it very easy to get lost, so bring a snack and some extra water, just in case.

To begin this hike, start to the left of the Cape Ann Sportsman's Club, and walk 0.25 mile to a second gate, where you will see a gravel pit on the right. Walk around the gate and continue on Dogtown Road. This wide path winds gently through a combination of hilly pastures and reforested land. As the path continues, keep an eye out for Dogtown Square, which is identified by the carving "DT SQ" on a rock on the right side of the trail.

Where Dogtown Road forks at Dogtown Square, take a right up the old cart road. This path winds among the trees. Along the way, you might notice additional small paths that jut off to the right and left. Follow one of these paths, and you may be fortunate enough to find one of Babson's Boulders. Millionaire philanthropist Roger W. Babson hired immigrant stonecutters to inscribe approximately two dozen boulders with words of inspiration during the Great Depression.

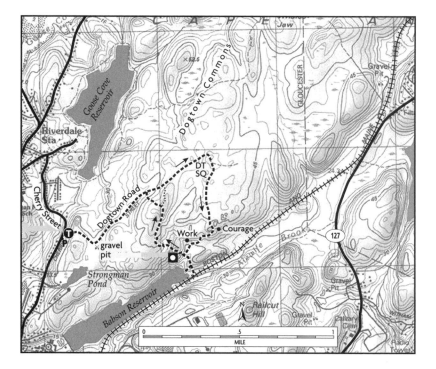

As you continue along the trail, take your time to explore. Keep an eye out for inscriptions such as "Kindness" and "Courage." After you pass "Work" on your right, turn to the right. This path is a field of boulders, and your pup will enjoy jumping from rock to rock. Eventually this path will intersect Dogtown Road. Turn left there to return to your vehicle.

2. Ravenswood Park

Location: Gloucester
Distance: 2.5 miles round-trip
Hiking time: 1.5 hours
Elevation gain: Negligible
Maps: The Trustees of Reservations; USGS Gloucester
Contact: The Trustees of Reservations, (978) 526-8687
Pet policy: Dogs must be leashed in the parking area and leashed or under voice control in the park.

Getting there: From Route 128, take exit 14 and follow Route 133 east toward Gloucester for 3 miles until it dead ends into Route 127. Turn right onto Route 127 and continue 2 miles to the park entrance and parking area on the right.

Ravenswood Park, enjoyed for more than a century by residents of Gloucester and surrounding towns, offers a peaceful place for an outing, with almost 10 miles of trails and carriage paths. This mixture of woodlots, old pastures, and swamp was originally owned by businessman and philanthropist Samuel Sawyer. Upon his death in 1889, Sawyer left the land with an endowment and instructions that the park "be laid out handsomely with drive-ways and pleasant rural walks." Ravenswood Park retains its originally intended ambiance and remains a fine place to take a hike with your dog.

From the trailhead, follow the wide gravel path called the Old Salem Road. To the left you will see a trail that leads to the Great Magnolia

Magnificent views of Gloucester Harbor

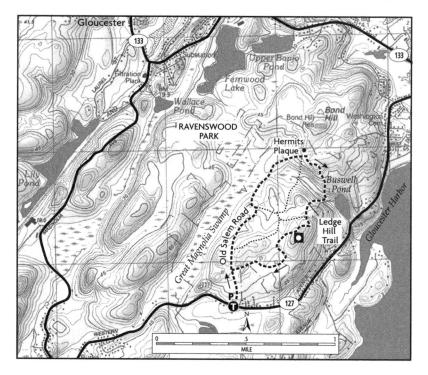

Swamp, home to native sweetbay magnolias (*Magnolia virginiana*). Continue along until you reach a V in the road. Continue to the left on Old Salem for a little less than a mile, until you reach a plaque that marks the spot in the woods where naturalist Mason "The Hermit" Walton built his cabin in the 1880s. Walton was thought to have lived in the woods for thirty-three years, spending his days studying the wildlife and writing.

After passing the plaque, continue to marker 22 and turn right on the narrow Ledge Hill Trail. You and your dog will enjoy weaving through the glacial erratics, boulders that were left in this area at the end of the last ice age. After marker 21, your pup can sip from the stream that leads to Buswell Pond. At marker 12, make sure your dog stays close to the trail, as it directly abuts private property.

Continue following the Ledge Hill Trail. Soon you will reach a cleared area with a fantastic view of Gloucester Harbor. You and your dog can take a break on the bench and watch the sailboats and other ships pass by. When you are ready, continue along the path until it reconnects with Old Salem Road. Turn left, and within 0.25 mile you will be back at the parking area.

3. Appleton Farms Grass Rides

Location: Hamilton, Ipswich
Distance: 3 miles round-trip
Hiking time: 1.5 hours
Elevation gain: Negligible
Maps: The Trustees of Reservations; USGS Ipswich
Contact: The Trustees of Reservations, (978) 356-5728
Pet policy: Dogs allowed off leash, subject to The Trustees of Reservations Green Dogs Program. All other dogs must be leashed.
Special notes: Admission is free to members of The Trustees, $3 daily use fee for non-members. Dogs are not allowed in the adjacent Appleton Farms.

Getting there: From Route 128, take exit 20N, then follow Route 1A north for 4.5 miles. Turn left onto Cutler Road and follow it for 2.2 miles. At the intersection with Highland Street, turn right. The parking area (twenty vehicles) is immediately on the right.

Older trees provide welcome shade at Appleton Farms Grass Rides.

Renowned for its miles of "grass avenues" bordered by woods, Appleton Farms Grass Rides has welcomed dogs and their owners for more than thirty years. Due to its increasing popularity, The Trustees of Reservations has implemented a Green Dogs Program that requires a free (to members) dog-walking permit in exchange for agreeing to follow the Grass Rides dog etiquette. The pilot program allows responsible owners to walk their dogs leash free.

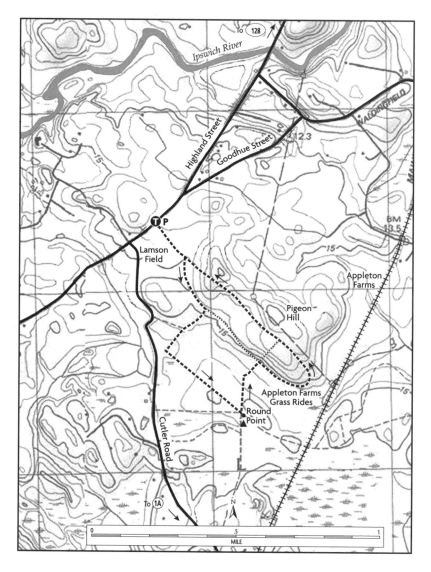

Appleton Farms Grass Rides offers a varying landscape of forest, open fields, and wetlands. Said to be the oldest continuous working farm in operation in the United States, planting began in 1638. The Grass Rides were gifted to the Trustees in 1970 by some of the descendants of Thomas Appleton, the original owner. A series of crisscrossed loops forms the network of trails. Even though the trails are defined, it is very easy to get turned around or temporarily lost. Bring a flashlight if you are hiking in the late afternoon, and always allow for more time than you think you will need. The wide-open and smooth trails of the Grass Rides make it a great place to visit with your dog year-round.

Grab a map at the interpretive area, then cross through the hay fields under a canopy of some large old trees. Once you have entered the woods, cross over a large path perpendicular to the one you are on now. Continue straight into the woods, and turn right at the next intersection. Follow this path as it winds its way back toward Cutler Road. Just before reaching the road, turn left. This path will bring you to Round Point.

Five rides (as such trails are called in England) converge like the spokes of a wagon wheel at this central clearing. You will know you are there when you see a large, granite pinnacle. Salvaged from the demolition of Gore Hall (the former Harvard College Library), the large granite object was positioned at Round Point in 1914.

To continue, look back and take the trail directly to the right of the one that you took to Round Point. When you reach another four-way intersection, turn right on a trail heading southeast. This trail will turn gently in the opposite direction and will bring you back toward your vehicle.

4. Bald Hill Reservation

Location: Boxford, Middleton, North Andover
Distance: 3.5 miles round-trip
Hiking time: 1.5 to 2 hours
Elevation gain: 120 feet
Maps: Boxford Trails Association/Boxford Open Lands Trust; Essex County Greenbelt Association; USGS Reading; USGS Lawrence
Contact: Department of Conservation and Recreation, (978) 369-3350; Boxford Trails Association/Boxford Open Lands Trust, (978) 887-7031; Essex County Greenbelt Association, (978) 768-7241
Pet policy: Dogs must be leashed.

Special notes: Hunting is permitted in season on some sections of this property; contact the Department of Conservation and Recreation for additional information.

Getting there: From Interstate 95 north, take the Endicott Street/ Boxford exit. Turn left, and from the exit ramp drive 0.2 mile. Turn right onto Middleton Road and travel 1.6 miles to park at the pullout on the left by a small reservation sign.

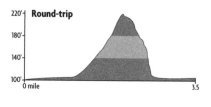

Bald Hill Reservation is one of Essex County's best places to take an outing with your dog. The Commonwealth and the Essex County Greenbelt Association have protected over 1800 contiguous acres, which include the John C. Phillips Wildlife Sanctuary, Boxford State Forest, and Boxford Woodlots. This conserved land contains a fine collection of forests,

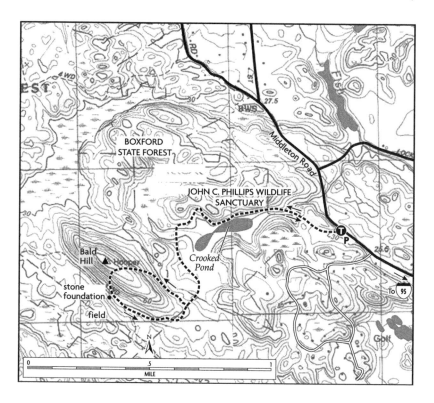

Tasman meets a friend at Bald Hill Reservation.

wetlands, ponds, streams, and open fields in which you and your furry friend can frolic. Migratory birds and wildflowers in spring, fall foliage, and winter tracking make visiting this property worthwhile at any time of year. Take a morning or the whole day to explore this fantastic place.

From the parking area, follow the wide main path into the woods. Shaded by the large hemlock trees, this trail continues along a low-lying swamp. Soon you will cross a cool, clear stream where your dog might enjoy a drink. The trail then continues along the shore of Crooked Pond. Beavers frequent this area, so—depending on the day and beaver activity—the main trail can often be quite wet. Bring sturdy boots, and keep an eye out for informal trails that allow you to avoid the water, even if your dog may not want to oblige you.

At the end of Crooked Pond, the trail will pass near a large beaver dam. Planks of wood have been placed on the trail for safe passage, but use your judgment of the height and flow of the water to determine if you can cross safely. As you continue, you will pass a small trail on your left, and the main trail will begin a gentle but steady climb to the top of

Bald Hill. At marker 12, take a right on the trail that will lead you and your dog on a walk to the summit.

At the top of the hill you will find an open meadow. Although the view isn't much, this area is perfect for a picnic or a round of fetch on a sunny day. About halfway across the meadow, turn left on a trail that will lead you down to the base of the hill and to another open field. Here you will find an old fireplace and remnants of the stone foundation of the Russell–Hooper farmhouse. Stone walls found in this area are a reminder of the people who once settled and farmed this land.

To continue, turn left at the stone fireplace and follow the trail as it skirts the base of the hill. Keep alert for signs of deer along the trail. When you reach marker 12, you can retrace your steps back to the parking area and your vehicle.

5. Weir Hill Reservation

Location: North Andover
Distance: 2.5–3 miles round-trip
Hiking time: 1.5 hours
Elevation gain: 190 feet
Maps: The Trustees of Reservations; USGS Lawrence
Contact: The Trustees of Reservations, (978) 682-3580
Pet policy: Dogs must be leashed or under voice control.
Special notes: Lake Cochichewick is part of the Town of North Andover's public drinking water supply; swimming is not allowed.

Getting there: From Interstate 93 north, take Route 125 north for 7.3 miles. Merge left onto Route 114 west. At the traffic light opposite Merrimack College, turn right onto Andover Street and follow it for 0.2 mile. Turn right at the traffic light at Pleasant Street and

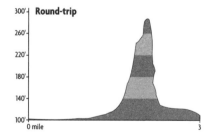

follow it for 0.6 mile. Bear right at a fork and continue 0.2 mile to the intersection at Old North Andover Center. Go straight for over 0.1 mile and then left onto Stevens Street. Continue for 0.8 mile to the entrance on the right. Roadside parking is limited.

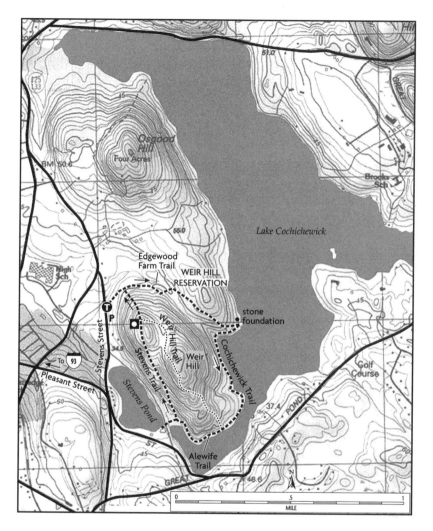

Gentle slopes and scenic vistas of Lake Cochichewick make Weir Hill (historically pronounced "wire hill") a great place to visit. Because of its unique history, Weir Hill supports a patchwork of ten types of plant communities, including a 60-acre oak-hickory forest, wet meadows, intermittent streams, and a wide range of wildflowers. With 4 miles of hiking trails, it is a popular destination for dogs and their owners, but it is quite common for hikers to travel solo on the trails, which offer a serene place to spend an afternoon.

From the parking area, grab a map from the visitor display and take the wide path heading uphill. The Stevens Trail will veer to your right, but stay to the left on the Edgewood Farm Trail. Your pup will enjoy jumping over rocks and roots and wading in a small stream as you make your way down to the lake.

When you reach an old foundation, continue to the right, following the shoreline on the Cochichewick Trail. Note: Lake Cochichewick is part of the Town of North Andover's public drinking water supply, so there is no swimming allowed. But don't fret; the adjacent Stevens Pond is just around the bend and a great spot for a dip!

As the trail continues along the lake, on the right you will reach the Weir Hill Trail, which bisects the reservation. Rather than heading uphill, continue straight onto the Alewife Trail.

At the southern edge of the forest, you will reach Stevens Pond, which offers a good place to take a swim. After enjoying a few laps, head back to the main trail and turn left onto the Stevens Trail, which steadily climbs to the top of a drumlin (an elongated hill of glacial drift) directly adjacent to Weir Hill. The meadow on this hilltop was once used for grazing cows

Wide trails at Weir Hill Reservation

and sheep and now offers a great place to soak up some sun and stop for a doggie biscuit break. Enjoy the shade of the large oak trees as you continue on this path back to your vehicle.

6. Deer Jump Reservation

Location: Andover
Distance: 2–6 miles round-trip
Hiking time: 1 to 3 hours
Elevation gain: Negligible
Maps: The Andover Village Improvement Society; USGS Lawrence
Contact: The Andover Village Improvement Society, www.avisandover.org (no phone)
Pet policy: Dogs must be leashed or under voice control.

Getting there: From Interstate 93, take exit 45 to River Road, toward South Lawrence. In just over a mile, turn right on Launching Road. Continue until you see a sign for Deer Jump Reservation on the right. Park on the right side of the road.

This long, narrow property provides scenic vistas and miles of trails along the Merrimack River. Deer Jump Reservation has long been a natural retreat for humans and animals alike, with its large groves of hemlock and pine and the cool waters of Fish Brook. According to the Andover Village Improvement Society (AVIS), a great horned owl nest has been observed within the reservation, while red foxes, turkeys, white-tailed deer, and great blue herons are commonly seen. With lots of access to the river and few people on the trails, this reservation will be a favorite for you and your pooch.

From the parking area, begin on a smooth, wide path that leads down to the river. The trees, including paper birch, maple, ash, and beech, are abundant. In this section of river, the slope down to the water can be quite steep. Once at the river, turn right on a trail that meanders along the shore for about 0.5 mile. Soon you will reach a clearing in the woods and a pumping station at the end of Fish Brook. Turn right, heading away from the Merrimack, and look for a bridge heading left across the brook. The trail then returns to the river, and continues for about a mile. Pine Island is off to the left in the middle of the river.

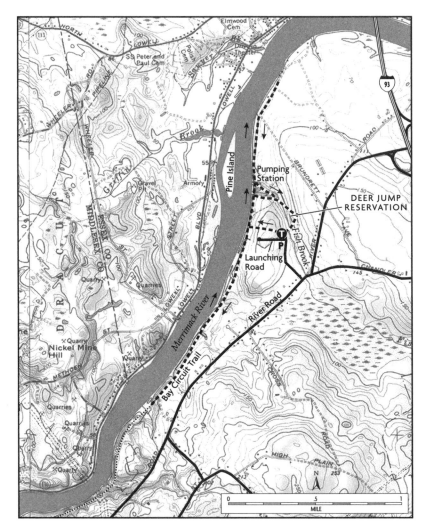

To return, retrace your steps to Fish Brook. After crossing it, follow the brook upstream until you reach a stone wall. Turn right, and then left on a trail that will lead you back to your vehicle.

To lengthen your hike, continue from Fish Brook and retrace your steps to where the original trail met the river. The trail then continues in the opposite direction for almost 4 miles. This section of trail is part of the regional Bay Circuit Trail, which connects the reservation to downtown Lowell. Much of this trail is abutted by private property, so make sure that the pooch stays close.

A small sign marks the entrance to Deer Jump Reservation.

7. Ward Reservation

Location: Andover, North Andover
Distance: Main trail, 4 miles round-trip; Bog Trail, 0.5 mile round-trip
Hiking time: 2 to 2.5 hours
Elevation gain: 180 feet
Maps: The Trustees of Reservations; USGS Lawrence
Contact: The Trustees of Reservations, (978) 682-3580
Pet policy: Dogs must be leashed.
Special notes: Open year-round, 8:00 AM to sunset

Getting there: From Interstate 93 north, take Route 125 (exit 41) north 5 miles. Turn right onto Prospect Road and follow it for 0.3 mile to the entrance and parking area on the right.

Ward Reservation's solstice stones

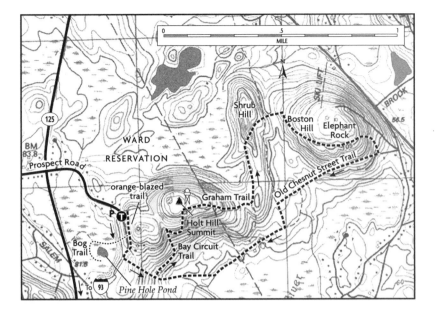

With amazing views of the city, miles of shaded trails, and a quaking bog, Ward Reservation is a great place to visit with your dog. A conglomerate of more than forty separate parcels of former farm and pasture land have been combined to make this 695-acre reservation with over 13 miles of trails, 17 miles of stone walls, and three hills (Shrub Hill, Boston Hill, and Holt Hill). The focal point of the Ward Reservation is 420-foot Holt Hill, the highest point in Essex County.

To begin this hike, start from the parking area, pass a small private home on your left, and take the orange-blazed trail heading south. Follow your dog through a patch of woods and a small orchard, then pass another private residence on your left. Don't worry—you are not trespassing—but make sure the pooch is polite as you walk through the open field and enter the woods. When you intersect with the green-blazed trail, follow it in a northerly direction toward Holt Hill. The green trail is also known as the Bay Circuit Trail. First conceptualized in 1929 as an outer "emerald necklace," the Bay Circuit is a trail in progress. When complete, the main line of trail will extend 200 miles through thirty-four towns in eastern Massachusetts from Kingston Bay to Plum Island and will link the parks and open spaces surrounding metropolitan Boston.

When you reach the top of Holt Hill, take a moment to enjoy the views of the Boston skyline and the Blue Hills. While on the summit, you may notice an interesting arrangement of stones in the shape of a compass. Known as "solstice stones," these narrow slabs mark the location of the sun for the summer solstice (around June 21), spring equinox (around March 21), autumn equinox (around September 21), and winter solstice (around December 21).

Once you have soaked up the sun, head east and down the hill on the blue-blazed trail, also known as the Graham Trail. This trail is a loop, so when you reach the first intersection, stay to the left and continue straight. A few trails will enter on the left, as you skirt the base of Shrub Hill. Staying on the blue-blazed trail, continue toward the top of Boston Hill. There you will find Elephant Rock, appropriately named for its grayish hue and wrinkled sides. Enjoy the views to the east of the North Shore from Gloucester to Boston. Heading steadily downward, continue on this loop until you reach the Old Chestnut Street Trail (orange-blazed trail), where you will turn left. Follow south and then west, all the way back to your vehicle.

If your pup wants more, take fifteen minutes and check out the quaking bog. Just before reaching the parking area on the orange-blazed trail, turn left on the Bog Trail. If you are interested in learning more, grab the nature walk interpretive guide that you will find at a small kiosk. The wooden boardwalk seems to be floating, but underneath you is a mat of vegetation resting on the accumulation of more than 19 feet of muck. As you continue your walk, observe the lush vegetation, including cattail, highbush blueberry, cinnamon fern, cranberry, and cotton grass. In less than a half mile you will reach Pine Hole Pond. It may look tempting, but don't allow your dog to swim here. When you are done exploring this unique place, retrace your steps back to the parking area.

8. Lynn Woods

Location: Lynn
Distance: 2.75 miles round-trip
Hiking time: 1.5 to 2 hours
Elevation gain: 180 feet
Maps: City of Lynn; USGS Lynn
Contact: Lynn Woods Park Ranger, (781) 477-7123; City of Lynn, www.ci.lynn.ma.us
Pet policy: Dogs must be leashed.

Special notes: The ponds provide the drinking water for the residents of Lynn and surrounding communities, so swimming is not allowed.

Getting there: From Route 128, take exit 44 to Route 129 East. Follow Route 129 for 3 miles, and then turn right onto Great Woods Road. Parking is at the end of the road next to the ball field.

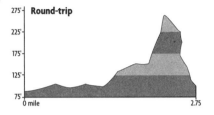

At nearly 2200 acres, Lynn Woods Reservation is one of the largest municipal parks in the United States. The forest contains a variety of ponds, wetlands, swamps, streams, large glacial outcroppings, and rocky ledges. Wildlife is abundant, including over a hundred species of birds that either inhabit or seasonally frequent the woods. You often can see hawks, owls, foxes, and deer while walking the trails. Lynn Woods truly feels wild in the city.

Before visiting Lynn Woods print out the great map found on the City of Lynn's website. All official roads and trails are numbered using a grid system, which makes the navigation of the forest much easier

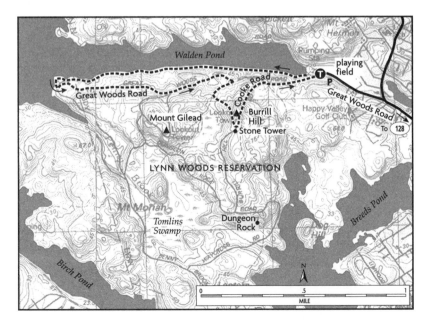

with map in hand. From the parking area, continue past the gate on the now-gravel Great Woods Road. Within a few minutes, take the first trail to the right and head down toward Walden Pond. This forested trail skirts the southern edge of the pond. Rocks and roots crisscross the trail, and a smattering of boulders makes for some interesting detours along the way.

The Stone Tower, Lynn Woods

In just over a mile, this trail reconnects with Great Woods Road, and you turn left. This wide gravel road is higher in elevation than the trail along the water and provides great views of Walden Pond. It's also relatively smooth and steady, which makes it a good trail to walk with an older dog. As you continue, various paths will veer to the right and back into the woods. If you have a full day to explore, you can head south and search for pirate treasure at Dungeon Rock or explore Tomlins Swamp.

Continuing on Great Woods Road, look for a small blue sign on a tree showing "D5-6," where you turn right and begin your ascent of Burrill Hill (285 feet). At D5-5, turn left on a trail that will lead you to the summit. The trail is steep at times, but steps have been built into the hillside to aid in your travel. Found at the top of the hill is the 48-foot Stone Tower, which was constructed under the auspices of the Works Progress Administration (WPA) in 1936. Set on the highest point in Lynn, the tower was built for fire observation and to provide shelter for the work crews. Views from this area are impressive, including Lynn's waterfront, the Boston skyline, and beyond.

Once you are done enjoying the scenery, continue to the left down Cooke Road. This wide gravel path will reconnect with Great Woods Road. Turn right to return to your vehicle.

9. Breakheart Reservation

Location: Saugus
Distance: 2.7 miles round-trip
Hiking time: 1.5 to 2 hours
Elevation gain: 200 feet
Maps: Department of Conservation and Recreation; USGS Boston North
Contact: Department of Conservation and Recreation, (781) 233-0834; Friends of Breakheart Reservation, (781) 710-3129
Pet policy: Dogs must be leashed with the exception of Bark Place, an off-leash dog park.
Special notes: In summer, the 2-mile-long Pine Tops Road is open to vehicles. In addition, the supervised swimming area at Pearce Lake draws crowds. For best hiking conditions, visit during the off-season.

Getting there: From Interstate 95, take exit 44 to Route 1 south. Head south for 2.5 miles, and take the Lynn Fells Parkway exit. Continue for 0.3 mile, and turn right onto Forest Street. In another 0.3 mile, find parking near park headquarters.

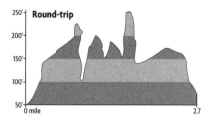

With hardwood forests, two lakes, seven rocky outcroppings, and a rambling section along the Saugus River, the 640-acre Breakheart Reservation is loved by many a dog from the Boston area. The natural resources that are part of the reservation were once utilized by Native Americans to provide shelter, tools, and food. A miserable Civil War soldier stationed at this isolated location gave the park its current name. Today, an extensive trail system through the woodlands offers a variety of hiking opportunities, and an off-leash dog park named Bark Place provides an area for socializing with doggie friends.

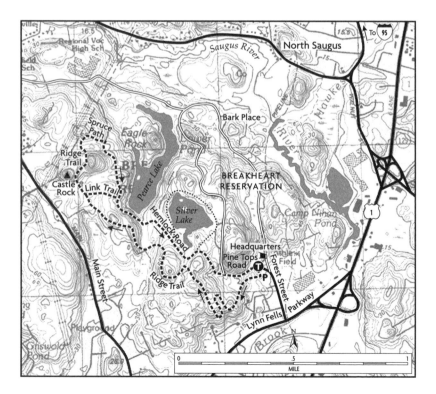

Higher ground affords nice views at Breakheart.

Before hitting the trails, stop at reservation headquarters to pick up a map and information. To begin the hike, head left on Pine Tops Road. During the off-season this road is closed to vehicles, which makes for a much more pleasant walk. Turn left on the white-blazed Ridge Trail, where oaks and maples line the trail. The trail will cross the Ash Path. Ascend one of the first rocky outcroppings on this trail for a stunning view of the Boston skyline. Descend and cross the Ash Path again, as the trail continues up a ridgeline that clears and offers a wider overlook.

Heading down, traverse a swampy area over a series of boardwalks. To the right, the Link Trail offers the opportunity for a shorter loop. For those who choose to continue, ascend another rocky section, following the white blazes. A trail to the left (0.1 mile) leads to the top of 286-foot-high Castle Rock, where you will find a vista from the highest point within the reservation. Back on the Ridge Trail, continue until you turn right onto the Spruce Path. Pass through a fire gate and onto paved Hemlock Road.

Hemlock Road is closed to traffic and is quite idyllic, offering a smoother surface for your dog's paws. Traveling south, catch a glimpse of Pearce Lake to the left. Look for a fire road on the left that will bring you to the upper pond, known as Silver Lake. A pleasant side trail skirts the circumference of the lake, providing access to the water's edge. Continue on Hemlock Road, which meets Pine Tops Road at 2.5 miles into this hike. Turn right to reach your vehicle.

If you're interested in checking out Bark Place, walk (or drive depending on the time of year) to the Pine Tops picnic area. Built as a cooperative effort between the Department of Conservation and Recreation and the Friends of Breakheart by reclaiming an abandoned parking lot, Bark Place provides an off-leash dog-play environment in an area surrounded by tall hemlocks. Benches are provided for weary owners, along with Mutt Mitts for picking up doggy deposits.

10. Middlesex Fells Reservation: East Side

Location: Malden, Medford, Stoneham
Distance: 2.2 miles round-trip
Hiking time: 1.5 hours
Elevation gain: 110 feet
Maps: Friends of the Middlesex Fells Reservation; USGS Boston North
Contact: Department of Conservation and Recreation, (617) 727-1199; Friends of the Middlesex Fells Reservation, (781) 662-2340, www.fells.org
Pet policy: Dogs must be leashed.

Getting there: To the east side of the Middlesex Fells, take Interstate 93 north to exit 33 (Route 28 north). Follow Route 28 for 0.4 mile and turn right onto Elm Street. Go three-quarters of the way around the rotary and head north on Woodland Road. Park at the Flynn Memorial Rink.

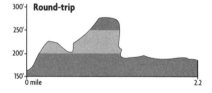

For those of us who yearn for the mountains yet find ourselves stuck in the urban jungle, this trail provides a great alternative to the regular after-

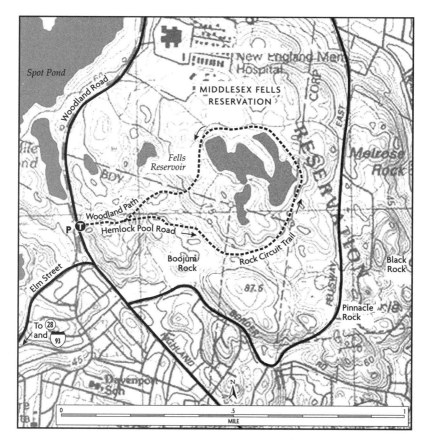

noon walk around the block. Just 9 miles north of downtown Boston, the Middlesex Fells Reservation offers a variety of trails, ranging from gentle strolls to more strenuous jaunts in the woods. Off the beaten path, this section of the Middlesex Fells provides generous views of the city and rugged trails that will put you and the pooch's legs to work.

Leash up at the parking area and walk north along Woodland Road. On the eastern side of the road is a metal gate, marking the entrance to the Fells. Carefully cross the road, and enter into the woods on the blue-blazed Woodland Path. This wide path meanders through the woods and passes Hemlock Pool on the right. This pond can get a bit swampy during the warm season but offers a good opportunity for a doggie drink. After passing the pond, take a right on Hemlock Pool Road. In spring, parts of this trail can become quite wet. Continue straight and take a right on the white-blazed Rock Circuit Trail.

This narrow rock- and root-laden trail winds continuously up and down through groves of birch and hemlock. You'll conquer a series of large granite outcroppings, and with each ascent the views become more beautiful. After passing an old rock foundation, the trail opens onto a large rock outcropping, a great place to stop for a break. From this spot on a clear day one can view the Boston skyline and the far-off ripple of the Atlantic Ocean.

After a water break, pick up the orange-blazed Rock Circuit Connector and head east and then north. Shilly Shally Brook and some wetlands offer another water break along the trail. Continue north, crossing over the Woodland Path, and pass through a chain-link fence. Follow the trail up a small hill. Turn right when you reach a fire road that encircles the Massachusetts Water Resources Authority

The eastern Fells offer great views of the Boston skyline.

(MWRA) Reservoir. **Note:** The reservoir is a backup water supply, so it's off limits to swimming.

Deer, coyotes, red-tailed foxes, and other animals frequent this area. Follow the trail around the reservoir, listening to the sound of bullfrogs. When you reach a gate, turn left on the Reservation Path. Pass a small wetland on the right, continue, and then reconnect with the white-blazed Rock Circuit Trail. Cross over Hemlock Pool Road, and then pass Shiner Pool on the right. When you reach the Woodland Path, turn right to retrace your steps back to Woodland Road and your vehicle.

11. Middlesex Fells Reservation: West Side

Location: Medford, Stoneham, Winchester
Distance: 2.2 miles round-trip
Hiking time: 1.5 hours
Elevation gain: 140 feet
Maps: Friends of the Middlesex Fells Reservation; USGS Boston North
Contact: Department of Conservation and Recreation, (617) 727-1199; Friends of the Middlesex Fells Reservation, (781) 662-2340, www.fells.org
Pet policy: Dogs must be leashed.

Getting there: To the west side of the Middlesex Fells, take Interstate 93 north to exit 33 (Route 28). Go north 1.8 miles to the Sheepfold entrance. Turn left and follow the road straight to the second parking lot.

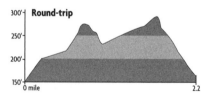

Open year-round, dawn to dusk, the Middlesex Fells Reservation's 2060 acres offer a welcome retreat for city dwellers. Fells is the Saxon word for rocky, hilly tracts of land, and it is an appropriate name for this scenic area. Rich in local history, the Middlesex Fells was once a favored area for timber, granite quarrying, and the ice industry. A variety of trails crisscross the reservation today, offering hiking opportunities for young dogs and old.

Stop at the kiosk adjacent to the parking area to have a look at the trail map. Having a map can come in handy on the trail, so it's a good idea to purchase one.

Take the trail from the parking area through the open space known as the Sheepfold. Often inundated with dogs, these fields can become overgrown in summer, so check for ticks during and after your hike. At

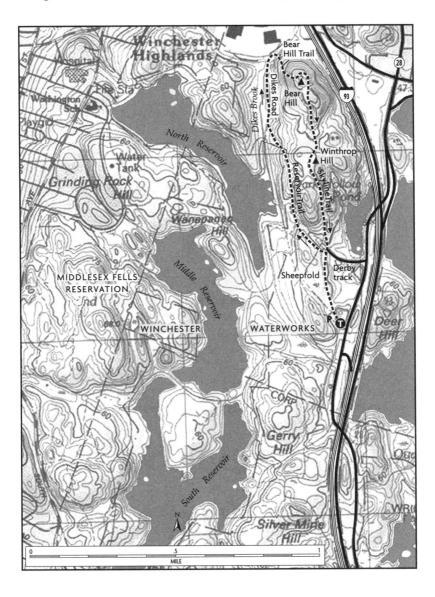

Dikes Brook provides a cool drink for dogs on a warm day.

the end of the fields, you will intersect the soapbox derby track, which was originally built in the 1950s. Turn left on this paved road. (Don't worry, no vehicles are allowed!) Continue until it ends, then make a slight left and join the orange-blazed Reservoir Trail.

This scenic trail overlooks the Middle and North Reservoirs found within the Fells. Although they're tempting, these bodies of water provide water to the town of Winchester and are off limits to swimming. Continue as this trail meanders through the forest, eventually dipping to Dikes Road. Turn right, and follow this trail as it runs parallel to Dikes Brook. When you reach an intersection, turn right and head up a rocky trail leading to the top of Bear Hill. When this trail intersects the blue-blazed Bear Hill Trail, turn right. From the tower on top of the 317-foot-high hill, you'll have 360-degree views of the Fells framed by the Boston skyline in the distance.

Once you're done soaking up the scenery, head downhill on wide Bear Hill Road. In just over a quarter mile, turn right into a small field.

This trail will connect to the white-blazed Skyline Trail. Take this trail left, heading south, and stopping for a moment to enjoy the view from the top of Winthrop Hill. This 291-foot-high hill provides a stunning overlook down over the reservoirs. Only the faint sound of the highway reminds you that you're near a large city.

The Skyline Trail continues down the hillside, becoming steep at times. At the bottom of the hill, turn right and then left to a trail that leads back to the open fields and your vehicle.

Want to hike longer? The west side of the Fells offers some great long-distance hiking. The following two trails can be picked up along this hike. Refer to your trail map for specifics.

Reservoir Trail: Orange Blaze

Distance: 5.2 miles

Hiking time: 3.5 hours

The Reservoir Trail encircles the reservoirs, though never along their shores. Much of it follows old carriage roads and is good for older dogs.

Skyline Trail: White Blaze

Distance: 6.9 miles

Hiking time: 5 hours

The mostly wooded Skyline Trail offers great views and several ascents, providing a great doggie workout for very active dogs.

NORTHWEST OF BOSTON

12. Dunstable Rural Land Trust Wildlife Preserve

Location: Dunstable
Distance: 2.25 miles round-trip
Hiking time: 1.5 hours
Elevation gain: Negligible
Map: USGS Townsend
Contact: The Dunstable Rural Land Trust, www.drlt.org
Pet policy: Dogs must be leashed or under voice control.

Getting there: The Dunstable Rural Land Trust Wildlife Preserve is located at 1076 Main Street in Dunstable. From Route 3 north, take exit 35 to Route 113 heading west. Continue on Route 113. From the center of Dunstable, continue straight on Main Street. In a few miles, you'll find a small parking area on the left side of the road, marked by a sign for the wildlife preserve.

The mission of the Dunstable Rural Land Trust (DRLT), founded in 1974, is focused on preserving, conserving, and educating people about the beautiful rural landscape that is Dunstable, Massachusetts. The 350-acre DRLT Wildlife Preserve, a testament to the nonprofit's efforts, provides trails through old-growth forest, along very active beaver ponds, and through open meadows. The property is linked to the Nashua River Rail Trail, which travels 11 miles through the towns of Ayer, Groton, Pepperell, and Dunstable. The preserve becomes a wonderland in winter, with opportunities for skiing, snowshoeing, and ice-skating.

From the parking area, continue past the gate on a wide footpath.

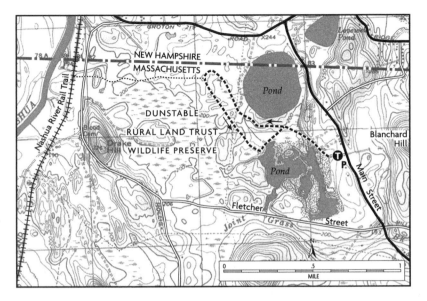

Walk down a small hill, and in a few minutes you will enter a large open area with a house up to the left. If your pup likes to wander, leash up through this area to be respectful of the private residence. Farther along, the path will open up, with a large meadow on the right and a pond on the left. Take a short detour down to the pond if your dog is ready for a swim.

Back on the main trail, the path follows a grove of pine trees on the left. White-tailed deer like to bed down with their young in this area. The path becomes shaded as you enter a larger stand of trees, then opens up into a second meadow. Beaver frequent this area, and you can often see signs of their activity along the trail. Continuing on the main trail, you'll find a small beaver pond ahead on the right. The trail then becomes sandy as you skirt the western edge of a larger pond that reaches all the way to the southern New Hampshire border.

At the far edge of the pond the trail diverges; the trail to the right eventually leads to the Nashua River Rail Trail. To continue, take the trail to the left as it loops back in a southerly direction. This sand and gravel trail meanders through a reclaimed gravel pit, where evergreen and deciduous trees now grow. Keep a watchful eye out for the occasional porcupine. Soon you will see a path that veers left into the forest. This

Opposite: Beavers hard at work

path will lead you back to the trail where you started. When you intersect the main trail, turn right to head back to your vehicle.

13. Groton Place and Sabine Woods

Location: Groton
Distance: 2.5 miles round-trip
Hiking time: 1.5 hours
Elevation gain: Negligible
Maps: New England Forestry Foundation; USGS Ayer
Contact: New England Forestry Foundation, (978) 952-6856
Pet policy: Dogs must be leashed or under voice control.

Getting there: From Interstate 495, take Route 119 (exit 31). Continue west for 7 miles toward Groton. In Groton Center, bear left on Route 225. Continue to follow signs for Route 225, and stay on this road for 1.5 miles. The turnoff for parking is on the left, and the entrance to the property is through a brick and iron gate.

The Groton Place and Sabine Woods property includes nearly 200 acres of forest and field to romp in and is managed by the New England Forestry Foundation. When combined with an adjacent property owned and managed by the Groton Conservation Trust, this open space includes more than 1800 feet of frontage on the east side of the Nashua River. The well-groomed walking trails zigzag through what was once farmland and forest and offer plenty of river access for water-loving pooches. In addition to magnificent white pine and plantations of other softwoods, you'll encounter two small ponds and extensive plantings of rhododendron, azalea, and other flowering shrubs.

From the parking area, enter the property through the large iron gate. Continue straight, until you reach an old stone horse trough and headstone in memory of the Groton Hunt. Bear right into the open field on a trail that leads toward the river. A good access point for swimming is found when you first reach the river. The trail continues to your left along the river, and in less than five minutes you will enter the woods. Keep your eyes and ears open, for it is very likely that you and your pup could cross paths with a horse and rider.

After walking for a few minutes in the deep shade of the woods, look to the right to locate a circular cement bench. This area, which includes one of the unique sculptures found on the property, marks where Frederic C. Dumaine and his beloved horse were buried. Mr. Dumaine, the former owner of this estate, was an avid foxhunter and dog lover. Guarding this final resting spot is a lifelike statue of a dog. As you continue your hike, follow the path through the woods of hemlock, spruce, and pine, and stop as often as your dog wants for another wade in the Nashua River. The Nashua River used to be one of the most polluted rivers in the country, until the community undertook a major volunteer effort to clean the river and conserve the land along its banks. Please help continue to protect water quality, and pick up after your pooch along the trail.

When you reach a boathouse, take the trail that heads left toward the Groton School. At this point, make sure your dog is leashed because

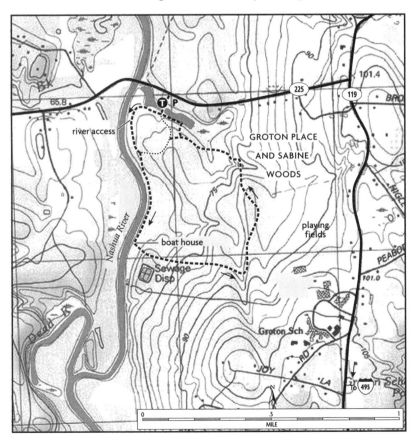

A stone sculpture guards the trails at Groton and Sabine Woods.

the adjacent school is private property. When you reach the playing fields, take the trail that heads to the left, and make your way back into the woods. Soon you will pass a sign for Sabine Woods, and as the trail continues you will see a stone wall on your right. Many little trails shoot off from your path, but if you stick to the trail most traveled you will eventually make your way back to your vehicle.

For water-loving pooches and owners interested in spending some additional time on the river, venture just up the road to Nashoba Paddler, which rents canoes and kayaks by the hour or the day. For directions or to make reservations, contact Nashoba Paddler at (978) 448-8699.

14. Spring Hill/Nashoba Brook Conservation Areas

Location: Acton
Distance: 4.5 miles round-trip; Nashoba Brook loop, 2 miles round-trip; Spring Hill loop: 2.5 miles round-trip
Hiking time: 2 to 3 hours
Elevation gain: Negligible
Maps: Acton Conservation Commission; USGS Maynard

Contact: Acton Conservation Commission, (978) 264-9631, www.actontrails.org

Pet policy: Dogs must be leashed or under voice control.

Special notes: This trail can get buggy as it is mostly shaded and wet. Be prepared and bring bug spray.

Getting there: From Route 2 in Acton, take Wetherbee Street north. Turn left on Route 2A/119, and then take a right on Pope Road. Take a left on Spring Hill Road, drive to the end, and park along the cul-de-sac.

With over 300 acres to explore, the Spring Hill and Nashoba Brook Conservation Areas are two hidden gems that you and your pup will greatly enjoy. The adjacent properties offer wildlife-viewing opportunities, stone walls, access to Nashoba Brook, and meandering trails under the cool shade of oak, maple, and birch trees. Picnic tables can be found at the Wheeler Road entrance of the Nashoba Brook Conservation Area.

Nashoba Brook

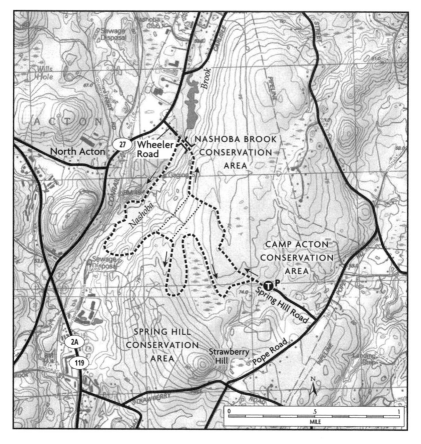

Begin the hike in the Spring Hill Conservation Area, but first take a moment to peruse the kiosk and map of the trails that can also be found on the Town of Acton's website. Take the red-blazed access trail to the main loop, which is blazed in yellow. Begin your loop by taking a right and walking in a northwesterly direction. Sections of this trail are part of the Bay Circuit Trail.

As you continue, a red-blazed trail will turn to the right in the direction of the Camp Acton Conservation Area. Stay straight on the yellow trail as it passes through a stone wall. Two blue-blazed trails bisect the Spring Hill loop, providing shorter loops for the senior dogs.

At the edge of the Spring Hill Conservation Area, watch for signs to pick up a red trail that cuts through a stone wall and connects to a yellow-blazed loop, now in the Nashoba Brook Conservation Area. Follow the trail to the right, crossing a bridge over Nashoba Brook.

The trail continues along the northern edge of the meandering brook. A few footbridges provide dry footing over mucky ground, but sturdy boots also come in handy. In spring, make sure to bring a towel as you can be assured that your dog will love to frolic through this area. Moving onward, keep an eye out for a blue-blazed trail that provides access to the southeasterly bank of the brook and the site of a nineteenth-century pencil factory. An education kiosk displays information about the history and ecology of the area.

Continue on the loop, until you see a red-blazed trail that reconnects to the Spring Hill Conservation Area. Turn right and then right again through a series of stone walls to return to the Spring Hill loop. The heavily shaded and often wet forest floor supports unusual plant communities, including mosses, partridgeberry, high-bush blueberry, and swamp azalea. The loop continues, passing through more stone walls and crossing some wetlands on a footbridge. Pass a blue-blazed trail on the left and head south. When the trail meets a red-blazed trail heading to Jay Lane, turn left, and then right on a yellow-blazed trail that will lead you to your vehicle on Spring Hill Road.

15. Great Brook Farm State Park

Location: Carlisle
Distance: 3 miles round-trip
Hiking time: 1.5 hours
Elevation gain: Negligible
Maps: Department of Conservation and Recreation; USGS Billerica
Contact: Department of Conservation and Recreation, (978) 369-6312
Pet policy: Dogs are allowed off leash under voice control, except near the visitor center and ice cream stand, where they must be leashed.
Special note: Parking at Great Brook Farm State Park costs $2.

Getting there: From Route 128, take exit 31B. Follow Route 225 west for 8 miles to the rotary in Carlisle center, then turn right on Lowell Road (following the sign to Chelmsford). The park entrance is 2 miles ahead on the right. When you reach North Road, turn right. The parking area is 0.5 mile ahead on the left.

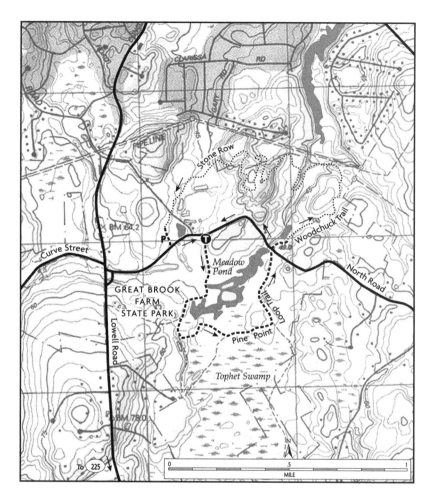

Great Brook Farm State Park is a reminder of what eastern Massachusetts agricultural landscape used to look like. An array of open fields, stone walls, dense woodlands, and historic buildings are iconic images of the past that still thrives today at this state park. Amid the beautiful scenery lie twenty miles of trails for you and your dog to enjoy.

Although the park offers endless trails to explore, the Pine Point Loop is a good place to take your dog on a fine summer day. As the name implies, while rambling around Meadow Pond much of the trail is well shaded by towering white pines.

Opposite: Toohey relaxes in a field at Great Brook Farm State Park.

From the parking lot, head left with your leashed dog along North Road until you see a sign for the Pine Point Loop Trail to the right. As soon as you are a safe distance away from the road, your pup can frolic off leash. Travel through a large open meadow, and turn right to start your walk around the pond. This trail is great for older dogs, as it is smooth and wide, making for easy-on-the-paws walking.

Stay on the main trail, passing a few wetlands and then some cornfields. This section of the state park was made for a picnic and is a good place to enjoy those treats you brought for you and your dog. To get closer to the water, take one of the smaller trails to your left. Your dog will find many great opportunities to swim. As the trail continues through some wetlands, a side trail heads south to Tophet Swamp. Eventually the Pine Point Loop reaches North Road, where you will find water tumbling out of Meadow Pond and over a dam. To get back to your vehicle, leash up, turn left, and walk for 0.5 mile back to the parking area.

If you are feeling a bit more adventurous and your dog has more energy to expend, cross over North Road and join the Woodchuck Trail. This weaves through the northern section of the property, crossing a few bridges along the way. Stone Row is another great trail to explore, but the many loops can leave you feeling a bit upside down. Bring a map, and don't be afraid to ask for directions.

16. Estabrook Woods/ Punkatasset Conservation Land

Location: Concord, Carlisle
Distance: 2–2.5 miles round-trip
Hiking time: 1 to 1.5 hours
Elevation gain: Negligible, 160 feet to top of Punkatassett Hill
Maps: Concord Conservation Commission; USGS Maynard
Contact: Concord Conservation Commission, (978) 318-3285
Pet policy: Dogs must be leashed or under voice control.

Getting there: From the center of Concord, take Monument Street north. Cross the Concord River and continue for 0.75 mile until you see a few small turnouts on the left side of the road, where you can park. The entrance to the woods is between 873 and 851 Monument Street.

With almost 1200 acres of woodlands, hills, ledges, and swamp, Estabrook Woods is a much-loved doggie destination. The Woods are a conglomeration of lands owned mostly by the town of Concord, a local land trust, and Harvard University. Rich with local history and frequented by writers and poets, the area was named "Easterbrooks Country" by Henry Thoreau. In addition, the woods are split by old Estabrook Road, which Minutemen hurried down to join the Concord fight at the North Bridge at the start of the American Revolutionary War.

Known mostly by the locals, Estabrook Woods is not well mapped or marked from the road. The Town of Concord owns the adjacent Punkatasset Conservation Land and has created a map outlining a loop trail

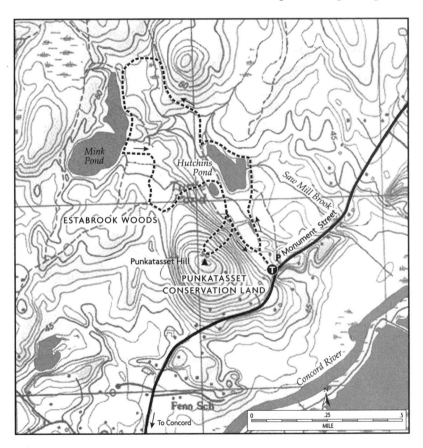

Muddy trails make for happy dogs at Estabrook Woods.

around Hutchins Pond and to the summit of Punkatassett Hill. For those who want to walk without the risk of getting lost, the route described here is a great way to explore the woods safely. For those who want a bit more adventure, a variety of trails crisscross through the woods. The easiest path to explore, Estabrook Road, bisects the woods and continues north all the way to Carlisle.

From the parking area, head down what looks like a private driveway to the entrance of the Punkatasset Conservation Land. A wooden kiosk displays a small map of the conservation land trails. From here, your dog will be happy to frolic leash free. Where the trail splits, stay to the right and follow the trail next to some large open fields on the right. Soon the path enters the woods and runs parallel to Hutchins Pond. A small beach provides great access for a quick paddle. Saw Mill Brook crosses over a spillway and leaves the pond to the right. Beaver are quite active in the area, so listen for the loud slap of their tails against the water.

At the end of the pond, stay to the left and follow the trail past an old orchard on your right. The smaller Mill Pond can be seen on your left. Cross a streambed, and then continue up a small hill as the trail passes through a series of stone walls. A trail diverges to the right, but continue to the left and past a large boulder. More boulders line the trail as you walk through another stone wall and creek bed. Depending on the time of year, the creeks can run dry. At the next intersection, a trail leads to the right in the direction of Estabrook Road. Continue to the left, on a trail that abuts the larger Mink Pond. In summer this pond, not as good a swimming hole as Hutchins, is often covered with water lilies in bloom. At a wooden log bench, the trail turns away from the pond.

At the next intersection, stay to the right as the trail passes though a swampy area. Looping around, the trail continues through a grove of evergreen trees that leave the trail covered with soft pine needles. This trail rejoins the Hutchins Pond loop. Turning right, the trail passes the open hillside of Punkatasset Hill. This is a popular sledding spot in winter and was once used as a ski slope. For a side trip, take the steep trail to the top of the clearing, and then turn left on a trail that loops back to the main trail. Passing through another open field, the trail then returns to the Punkatasset kiosk. Turn right and walk up the road and back to your vehicle.

17. Lincoln Conservation Land/ Mount Misery

Location: Lincoln
Distance: 3 miles round-trip
Hiking time: 1.5 hours
Elevation gain: Negligible
Maps: Lincoln Conservation Commission; USGS Maynard
Contact: Lincoln Conservation Commission, (781) 259-2612
Pet policy: Mount Misery has on-leash and off-leash trails. No more than three dogs are allowed per person. Dogs cannot swim outside of designated areas. Dogs must be leashed in the parking area.

Getting there: From Interstate 95 in Weston, take exit 26 (Route 20), and after 0.2 mile, take a left on Route 117 west. Continue for 7 miles to the parking area on the right.

Lincoln's 227-acre Mount Misery Conservation Land offers off-leash trails, hemlock forests, and access to the Sudbury River. According to folklore, the area received its name in the late 1700s after a pair of yoked oxen wandered up the hillside and wrapped themselves around a tree, ultimately causing their demise. Far from a miserable place, Mount Misery is a great place to spend a few hours walking with your dog.

Due to historical overuse from dogs, Lincoln has tightened its leash laws a bit and divided this property with on- and off-leash trails. Although that makes the area somewhat difficult to navigate with your dog, it's still worth a visit. Before hitting the trails, pick up the map created by the Lincoln Conservation Commission that clearly marks which trails are leash free. Along the trail, small signs will demarcate on- and off-leash sections.

From the parking area, walk with your leashed dog down a wide trail to the first swimming hole on this hike. A small beach makes a great access point to the water. After a swim, follow this trail straight along the northern edge of the pond. Watch for the turtles that like to bask in the

The Sudbury River is a popular spot for people and dogs alike.

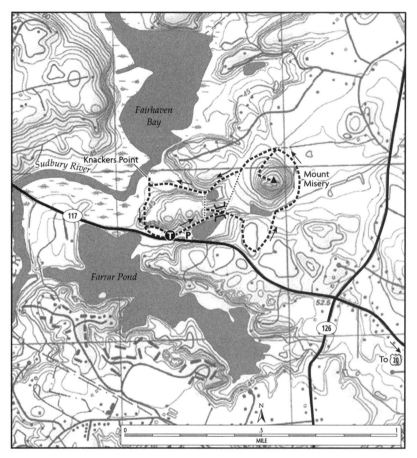

sun. After passing the pond, take a trail that leads to the right and cross on a wooden bridge over a small stream that feeds the pond below.

Turn left just before another pond on the right, although this one is not for swimming. At the next intersection turn right. The now off-leash trail skirts the base of Mount Misery. Follow this path until you see farm fields on your right, at which point turn left. Soon a trail to the top of Mount Misery will veer off to the left. The view from the top is less than spectacular, so if you prefer flatter ground continue straight to the next intersection and take a right onto a trail that leads down to the Sudbury River.

This smooth trail is adjacent to some wetlands, but don't fret if your dog wanders off into the muck: the river ahead offers clean cool water in which to wash off. Don't forget to pick up a few sticks along the trail if your dog enjoys a game of fetch. The trail ends at Knackers Point, where you'll find magnificent views of the Sudbury River and Fairhaven Bay. On a summer day you might run into some canoeists or kayakers who have pulled to shore for a picnic lunch.

From the river, you have a few options for returning to your vehicle. For the shortest route, turn right and then take your third left onto a trail that will lead you back to your vehicle. If you want to continue, refer to your trail map to further explore the various trails that loop through the woods.

18. Willards Woods

Location: Lexington
Distance: 1–1.25 miles round-trip
Hiking time: 45 minutes to 1 hour
Elevation gain: Negligible
Maps: Lexington Conservation Commission; USGS Maynard
Contact: Lexington Conservation Commission, (781) 862-0500
Pet policy: Dogs must be leashed or under voice control.

Getting there: From Route 128, take exit 32 to Middlesex Turnpike and head south. This road becomes Lowell Street. Turn right on Adams Street, and then right again on Hathaway Road. Take your first right on Brent Road, and follow as the road curves to the left and then to the right. When Brent Road takes a sharp right, find parking along the roadside. Additional but limited parking can be found on North Street. Wherever you decide to park, be respectful of neighbors and keep your dog on a leash until you have entered the woods.

This 100-acre property allows one to take a step back in time while wandering around an old farm that remains much as it was more than 140 years ago. You and your dog will enjoy exploring the site's many natural attractions, including a remnant apple orchard, open fields, a small pond, a tranquil pine grove, two brooks, and extensive wetlands. Large, scattered boulders exemplify this area's glacial history. Parts of this property can be wet, so be prepared with some boots for yourself and a towel for the pooch.

Willards Woods is used year-round by walkers, runners, cross-country skiers, and snowshoe enthusiasts, so remain alert on the trail and make sure your dog is under control when passing others. You will soon find that this place is very doggie friendly, as your pup can frolic through the fields and on the trails leash free.

Walk to the end of Brent Road, and enter the woods on your right. From the trailhead, head straight and in a minute or two you will cross Willards Brook. The water below is often quite mucky, so stay leashed in the beginning of this hike if your pooch likes the mud. The trail then turns right, bisecting a large open meadow. In summer the fields are filled with a variety of wildflowers and are home to many nesting birds. At the far edge of the field, the trail heads into the pleasant shade of a white

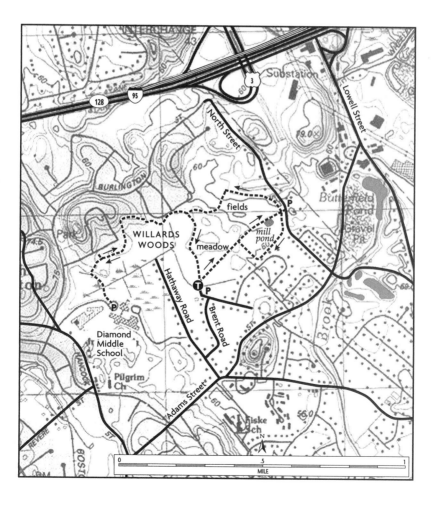

Wildflowers line the trails at Willards Woods.

pine forest. From here, you have the option of taking a variety of trails that loop through the woods and fields that make up Willards Woods.

At the next intersection, a trail leads to the right and loops around a historic mill pond. If you want to avoid the water, continue straight on a wide path between two stone walls. At the end of this path, the trail from the mill pond joins from the right. Turn left here into a large, open meadow. The trail skirts the northern edge of the fields, then crosses a brook on a wooden bridge. Continuing up a small hill, the trail passes through a stone wall. From here a variety of trails weave through the woods and back to the first meadow. For the shortest route, continue straight, but if you choose to walk a bit longer, turn to the right on a trail that also loops back. Once back at the first meadow, turn right and retrace your steps back to your vehicle. Not tired yet? Take the trail that leads to Diamond Middle School. This a dead-end trail with a series of boardwalks that cross over swampy area.

WEST OF BOSTON

19. Fresh Pond Reservation

Location: Cambridge
Distance: 2.5 miles round-trip
Hiking time: 1.25 hours
Elevation gain: Negligible
Maps: Friends of Fresh Pond Reservation Map; USGS Boston North
Contact: City of Cambridge Watershed Ranger, (617) 349-4793;
Friends of Fresh Pond Reservation, www.friendsoffreshpond.org
Pet policy: Fresh Pond is legally off leash for dogs belonging to
Cambridge residents only. All others dogs are allowed on a leash.

Getting there: From Route 2 and the Fresh Pond rotary, follow the Fresh
Pond Parkway (Route 2/Route 16) east toward Boston. The parking area
for Cambridge residents is on the right, adjacent to the Cambridge Water
Department. You will find two parking areas for Cambridge residents:
one just before the building and one after; nonresidents can get dropped
off, take public transit, or try to find parking in the adjacent shopping
mall or residential areas.

Fresh Pond Reservation consists of a large kettle-hole lake and about 162
acres of surrounding land. The retreating Laurentide Glacier sculpted the
area about 15,000 years ago. Native Americans were attracted to these
ponds, streams, woods, and marshes as they found an abundance of fish
and plentiful wildlife in this area. Fresh Pond today is part of a reservoir
system that supplies drinking water to the City of Cambridge, and for that
reason it is now fenced off to any human or canine use. The 2.25-mile
perimeter path is a popular place for recreation due to its scenic landscape

and proximity to the city. To avoid the crowds, visit during the week or in the early morning.

Start at the trailhead adjacent to the parking lot for Kingsley Park, where you will find a map of the trail and a doggie waste bag dispenser. Because this trail is so heavily used, it is important to pick up after your pet. To begin, follow the wide paved trail to the left, heading southwest. Soon you will pass a small meadow which in summer is filled with an assortment of wildflowers and offers a bench from which to enjoy the view.

Continue straight ahead as the trail enters a stretch shaded by large trees. If you are interested in taking the high road, look for a path that heads to the left and zigzags up the slope, then parallels the larger path below. You will encounter sweeping views of the reservoir from the higher trail. The trails reconnect adjacent to a golf course, so leash up if your furry friend is tempted by large green spaces. Keep alert for poison ivy that lines much of the fence along the trail. After about a mile you will find a newly designated doggie beach with water access to Little Fresh Pond. This is a great place for Fido to make new friends and cool off on a warm summer day.

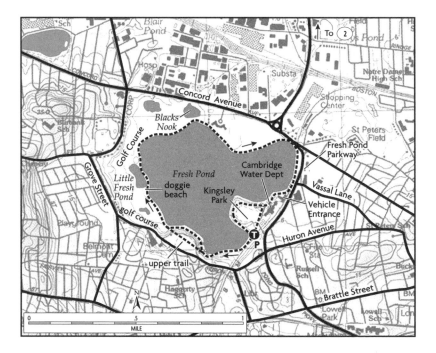

Time to frolic at the Little Fresh Pond dog beach

As the trail continues you will pass a few other smaller ponds and wetlands on your left. Take a detour to visit Blacks Nook and some of the more natural environments found within the reservation. As the path continues, it parallels Fresh Pond Parkway. To be safe, have your leash handy. Soon the trail will pass the Cambridge Water Department, where you will also find a water fountain and dog-friendly dish for a refreshing drink. Just past the fountain the path diverges. If you continue straight you will end back at the parking lot; if you want to go a bit farther, turn right on a trail that loops Kingsley Park and then returns to where you started.

20. Cat Rock Park

Location: Weston
Distance: 2 miles round-trip
Hiking time: 1.5 hours
Elevation gain: 180 feet
Map: USGS Framingham
Contact: Weston Conservation Commission, (617) 893-7320
Pet policy: Dogs must be under voice control. No more than three
dogs per person.
Special notes: Cat Rock is a popular dog-walking location. To avoid
the doggie crowds, visit in the early morning or evening.

Getting there: From Interstate 95, take exit 28 to Route 20 and head west. Turn right on School Street, then right on Church Street. Turn left on Route 117. Very shortly after, turn right on Drabbington Way. At the end of the road you will find parking next to a small playing field.

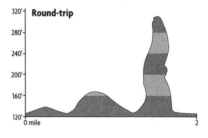

With nearly 130 acres to explore, Cat Rock Park is a place that you and your dog will want to return to again and again. Hobbs Brook runs through the park and supplies fresh water along the trail. Hobbs Pond offers a great spot for a dog paddle, and the 334-foot summit provides stunning views of the surrounding towns. This conservation area is a great place to visit year-round.

From the parking area, follow the path to the right of the ball field. When you meet the first intersection, turn right and cross Hobbs Brook on a wooden footbridge. Continue on this wide, smooth path under a canopy of large trees. When you reach an intersection marked by some larger rocks, follow the trail that continues to the left. This trail meanders, eventually bringing you down to a dam, a waterfall, and Hobbs Pond. The dam was originally built in 1957, and the cool, calm water is a refreshing break for your dog along the trail.

From the dam, head down a small incline to reach a bridge that crosses

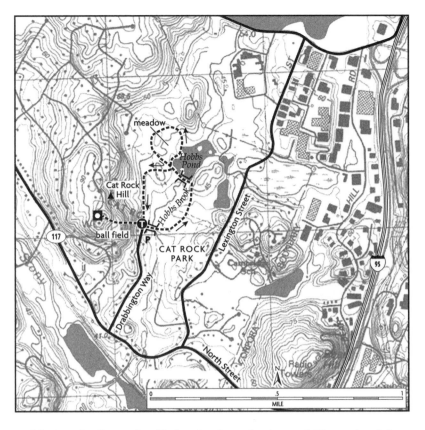

Hobbs Brook. The path will then lead you back up a hill, turning left to parallel the pond. Soon the trail will open up into a meadow adjacent to the southwestern edge of the pond. Take the trail to the right, making a loop around the meadow. A small side trail leads to the right down to the pond again, offering another opportunity for a swim and a view of the birds that frequent the area. Continue following the path around the perimeter of the meadow. Watch to your right for a small clearing in the brush and the trail that leads back into the woods.

The path passes through a stone wall and crosses an intermittent stream that often runs dry in the warmer months. The path in the woods widens and is well shaded by the trees that tower above. When you return to the first bridge at Hobbs Brook, turn right to take a path to the summit of Cat Rock Hill. The trail is rather steep, but the walk to the top takes no more than ten minutes.

This grassy hillside was once known as the Cat Rock Hill Ski Area. Run

In springtime, look for delicate and rare ladyslippers.

by the Town of Weston from 1957 to 1978, the ski hill had two rope tows with a slope for beginners and a more advanced run through the hemlock trees. Today, you will find a water tank at the summit and sweeping views of the towns that surround the peak. To return to your vehicle, walk down the open ski slope and retrace your steps back to your vehicle.

21. Weston Reservoir

Location: Weston
Distance: 2–2.5 miles round-trip
Hiking time: 1.5 hours
Elevation gain: Negligible
Maps: Weston Conservation Commission; USGS Framingham
Contact: Weston Conservation Commission, (781) 893-7320
Pet policy: Dogs are allowed on leash or under voice control.

Getting there: From Interstate 95, take exit 28 to Route 20, heading west. Turn left on Wellesley Street, and then right on Ash Street. Park on the right side of the road.

The Weston Reservoir Conservation Area is loved by many a dog and is a great place to walk with your pooch year-round. Although a fence prevents access to the reservoir, you will most definitely enjoy the beautiful views and the shade-covered trail that weaves through a dense pine forest.

From the parking area, leash up and look both ways before you cross sometimes-busy Ash Street. Once you get to the other side and far enough away from the road that you feel safe, your dog can explore this conservation area under voice control and leash free. The main path hugs the fence line, but to explore the path less traveled veer to the right through the open field until you reach a sign that reads "Watershed Protection Trail." This path runs parallel to the main path and remains cool even on warm summer days. In spring, lily of the valley and ferns grow abundantly along the trail's edge.

Just before the side trail reconnects to the main path, watch for a clear brook to your right where your dog might like to drink. A few intermittent streams like this one feed the reservoir along the way. When you

Tasman explores the meadow at Weston Reservoir.

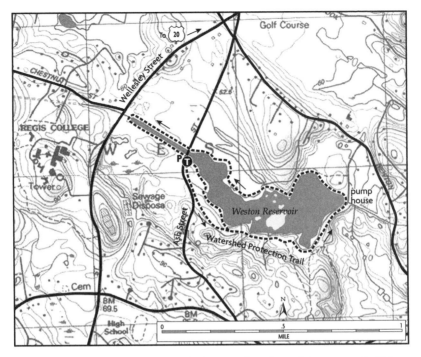

reach the main path, turn right following the edge of the reservoir. Take a break when you reach the pump house, where you will find a wide-open clearing and a great view back over the reservoir. Dogs often gather there for a shared frolic.

After enjoying the vista, continue on the trail as it skirts the other side of the reservoir. The trail becomes significantly wetter as it follows a low-lying wet area before reaching Ash Street. Be sure to bring bug spray in spring and summer. When you reach the road, leash up again before crossing. Your vehicle will be a walk of a few minutes up the road to your left.

If your pup wants more, you can go a bit farther. From the intersection of Ash Street, cross and look for a trail that continues on a 0.5-mile loop that will also bring you back to your vehicle.

22. Centennial Reservation

Location: Wellesley
Distance: 1.6 miles round-trip

Hiking time: 1 hour

Elevation gain: 200 feet

Maps: Wellesley Trails Committee; USGS Framingham

Contact: The Wellesley Natural Resources Commission, (781) 431-1019, x 294; Wellesley Trails Committee, www.wellesleytrails.org

Pet policy: Maximum of two dogs per person allowed on leash or under voice control. For additional dogs, request a permit from the Natural Resources Commission.

Special notes: Because of high grasses, ticks are prevalent in early summer and fall. Check yourself and your dog thoroughly after your hike.

Getting there: From Route 9 in Wellesley, turn on Oakland Street and follow the road south for 0.5 mile. Turn right at the sign for the Centennial Reservation and follow the partially paved road to the parking lot.

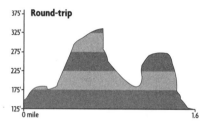

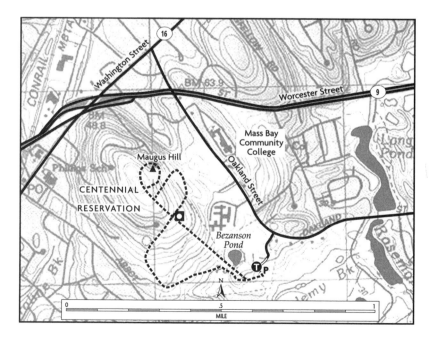

The woods at Centennial Reservation provide much-needed shade.

This wonderful reservation will allow you and pup to walk through open meadows and up Maugus Hill, which on a clear day will give you a view of rolling hills and the church steeples of surrounding towns. The property is divided by a variety of trails, so each time you visit there is a new one to explore.

Start your hike at the information board in the parking area, and continue straight down through the open meadow. Before reaching the pond, turn left up a hill, where the trail runs along the top of an esker. When the trail descends, take a right and cross a small footbridge, which leads into a large open field.

Continue straight and then slightly to the left as the trail begins to ascend the hill. The lower part of this area can get a bit mucky in spring; if that's the case, take the trail to your right and loop back to the main trail. Either way, continue up though the meadow and over to the left where the trail enters the woods. Now protected by shade, the trail meanders uphill through the woods. Passing one cutoff trail on your right, follow the main path as it continues upward and jogs slowly to the right. When you reach a wooden bench, take a short break and enjoy the view or continue on the trail to your left, which leads to the top of Maugus Hill (the highest point in Wellesley at 338 feet).

Just before the top of the hill, the trail turns right and heads down the hill toward Mass Bay Community College. Be alert, as this stretch of woodland is known to have a resident deer population. Before reaching the college parking lot, the trail swings back around and ascends slightly back to the top of the open meadow. From here, take the mowed trail all the way down the hill, and in summer look for milkweed and the beautiful monarch butterfly. At the bottom of the hill allow your dog a reward with a quick dip in Bezanson Pond. From the pond, follow the trail back to your vehicle.

23. Elm Bank Reservation

Location: Natick
Distance: 2 miles round-trip
Hiking time: 1 hour
Elevation gain: Negligible
Maps: Department of Conservation and Recreation; USGS Framingham
Contact: Department of Conservation and Recreation, (617) 333-7404
Pet policy: Dogs must be leashed, except along the nature trail, where they must be leashed or under voice control.
Special notes: The reservation is open year-round dawn to dusk; gates open at 8:00 AM.

Getting there: From Wellesley center, take Route 16 west for 1.7 miles. The Elm Bank Reservation will be on your left, marked by a green sign. To find the best parking for the trailhead, at the end of the driveway take a right and continue around the one-way loop road. You will pass multiple parking areas, but continue around the loop road following the exit signs. When you cross over a small stone-lined bridge, parking will follow on the right.

Elm Bank Reservation consists of 182 acres of woodlands, fields, and an old estate. The property is surrounded on three sides by the Charles River and provides a home for a variety of wildlife, including deer, which you might spot in the upland habitat near the river. Like the deer, your dog will greatly enjoy the northern section of the property, where numerous trails weave through the woods and along the river.

To find the trailhead from your parking spot, walk back along the roadway and cross the small bridge on foot. You will see a board with a trail map to your left. To begin your hike, walk on the main trail, with the Charles River on your left. Your dog will enjoy the smooth terrain and deep shade of the pine forest. Many places allow you to gain closer access to the river. If your dog enjoys swimming, your dog will love Elm

Dylan waits along the trail at Elm Bank Reservation.

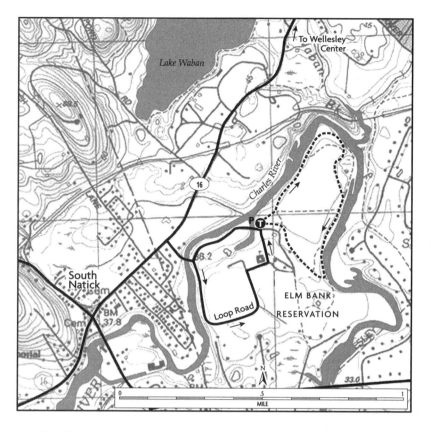

Bank! When you continue to the end of the peninsula, you will have a great 180-degree view of the river. Keep your eyes out for a great blue heron, turtles, and maybe even a muskrat in the water.

As you loop back, a number of trails break off into the woods. Feel free to explore these, as it is hard to get lost here: you always make your way back eventually to the river, where you can reorient, then make your way back to your vehicle.

24. Noanet Woodlands

Location: Dover
Distance: 3.5 miles round-trip
Hiking time: 2 to 2.5 hours
Elevation gain: 140 feet

Maps: The Trustees of Reservations; USGS Medfield
Contact: The Trustees of Reservations, (781) 784-0567
Pet policy: Dogs must be leashed in the parking area. Once within the woods, dogs can be leashed or under voice control.
Special notes: Dogs are not allowed in Caryl Park.

Getting there: From Boston, take Interstate 90 west to Route 128 south. Take exit 17 for Route 135 heading west. Turn left at the next traffic light on South Street. After 1 mile, turn left on Dedham Street.

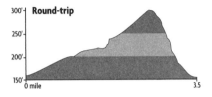

Continue for 2.2 miles to reach the entrance on the left. Since dogs are not allowed to enter from the main parking area due to its adjacency to Caryl Park, stop briefly to pick up a map at the ranger station. Then return to your vehicle, continue on Dedham Street, and park in the lot adjacent to the playing fields on the left.

Less than an hour away from the city, Noanet Woodlands is one of the area's best-kept secrets for hiking with your dog. The quiet surroundings, diverse environments, and spectacular views make these 695 acres a great place to visit year-round. Noanet Woodlands features three color-coded trails (yellow, blue, and red), and many intersections are marked with a number. The Trustees of Reservation map makes it much easier to navigate the network of trails.

From the parking area, leash up your dog and head into the woods to the right side of the playing fields. Once you're under the trees, a path will lead to the left in the direction of the Noanet Woods. This stretch of path is owned by the Town of Dover, so it is important to keep your dog on a leash. After crossing a small stream, continue until you reach a sign that marks the beginning of the Noanet Woods, where you will turn left.

Continue up a small hill. At the first intersection, stay to the right and follow the blue-blazed Peabody Trail, which leads to a couple of small ponds and a scenic waterfall. The Dover Union Iron Company once operated a mill here, and the preserved 24-foot-high dam and 20-foot-deep wheel pit give a glimpse into this area's historical past. The ponds are a great place to enjoy a snack or stop for a doggie paddle.

Opposite: Tasman checks out the waterfall at Noanet Woods.

To continue, take the trail between the two ponds. Joining the red-blazed Larrabee Trail, skirt the eastern edge of one of the ponds. In October the trail is illuminated by autumn leaves. When you reach trail intersection marker 18, turn right and back onto the Peabody Trail to cross Noanet Brook and then loop back around to the two mill ponds. At trail

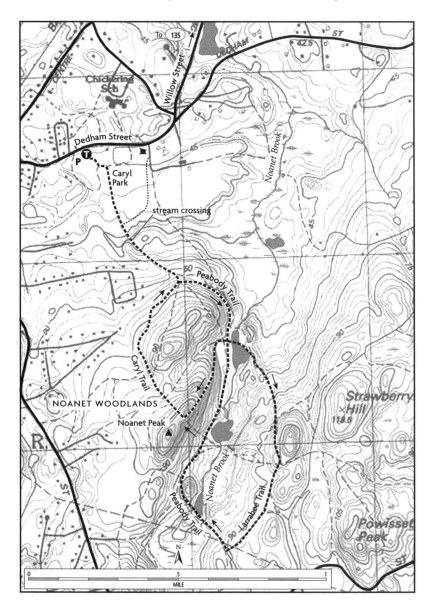

intersection marker 36, turn left and begin your ascent of 387-foot-high Noanet Peak. At the top, take a moment to enjoy the view of the Boston skyline and the adjacent Hale Reservation. The large rocky outcropping provides a great place to stop for a picnic lunch.

From the top, continue down the hill on a wide wood-chip trail. At trail intersection marker 6, pick up the yellow-blazed Caryl Trail. This trail is bordered by private residences on the left, so leash up if your dog likes to wander. At trail intersection marker 3, turn left to retrace your way back to your vehicle.

25. Rocky Narrows/Sherborn Town Forest

Location: Sherborn
Distance: 2.7 miles loop
Hiking time: 1.5 hours
Elevation gain: 130 feet
Maps: The Trustees of Reservations; USGS Medfield
Contact: The Trustees of Reservations, (781) 784-0567; Sherborn
   Forest & Trail Association, (508) 655-8157
Pet policy: Dogs must be leashed in the Rocky Narrows; dogs are
   allowed off leash or under voice control in the Sherborn Town Forest.
Special notes: A healthy population of white-tailed deer lives in the
   woods, so check carefully for ticks at the end of your hike.

Getting there: From the intersection of Routes 27 and 16 in Sherborn, follow Route 27 south. Turn left on Goulding Street, and then left on Forest Street. The parking area is on the right.

The wooded trails, scenic overlooks, and river access of the Rocky Narrows make this area an ideal place for you and your pooch to visit. Also known as the "Gates of the Charles," Rocky Narrows and the adjacent Sherborn Town Forest combined encompass over seven miles of trails. This natural area, which links to the Bay Circuit Trail, will have you coming back again and again.

From the parking area, grab a map and begin following the Red Trail to the right through open fields. The relatively easy path heads south and at marker 9 heads east, adjacent to some wetlands. At marker 10, head southeast as the trail runs parallel to the railroad tracks. Make sure that your dog is under control for this section of the walk. In about 0.25 mile you will reach marker 14, where you will turn right toward the first of two magnificent overlooks.

Dogs or their owners afraid of heights be warned as this narrow trail winds it way down to the river. From marker 18, turn to the right and make your way down to the canoe landing. On a quiet day, your dog will enjoy taking a few laps in the Charles River. After sunning a bit along the

The Charles River beckons.

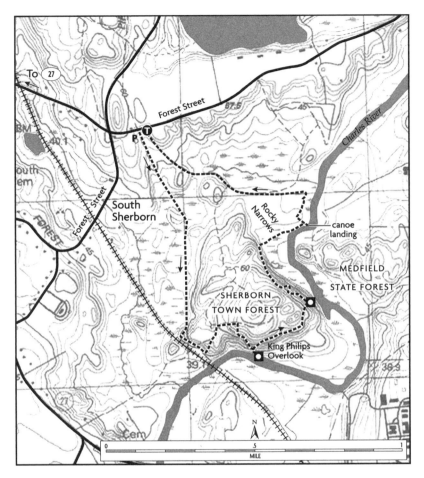

water's edge, take the trail leading to the right. At the next intersection, turn right, and then left at marker 20. The trail continues past some wetlands and some hills on the left. Turn right at marker 23 and walk through some fields and orchards before returning to your vehicle.

26. Callahan State Park/ Welch Reservation

Location: Framingham, Marlborough
Distance: 2.5 miles round-trip
Hiking time: 1.5 hours

Elevation gain: Negligible

Maps: Department of Conservation and Recreation; Sudbury Valley Trustees; USGS Framingham

Contact: Department of Conservation and Recreation, (508) 653-9641; Sudbury Valley Trustees, (978) 443-5588

Pet policy: Dogs must be leashed in the parking area; on trails, dogs should be leashed or under voice control.

Special notes: Callahan State Park is a very popular place to walk with dogs. To avoid the crowds, visit in the early morning or during the week. Part of this trail runs parallel with Baiting Brook and often can be quite muddy, so wear sturdy boots.

Getting there: Take Route 9 west to the Route 30 exit, then take a right at the first set of traffic lights on Edgell Road. Continue and take a left on Edmands Road. The parking area is a few miles farther on the left side of the road.

Located in the northwest corner of Framingham, Callahan State Park and the adjacent Welch Reservation provide over 800 acres of forest, fields, and about seven miles of well-marked trails to enjoy. This large open space is also used by equestrians, so watch out for horses and what they might leave along the trail.

Begin at the parking area and pick up a map at the kiosk, then take your leashed dog into the woods. Once away from the trailhead, your well-behaved pup is able to hike leash free. To begin your jaunt, take the Pipeline Trail. This wide path crosses over the Bay Circuit Trail and continues up a short, yet steep hill. The woods here are dense and provide welcome shade on warmer days. From the top of the hill, continue straight down, eventually reaching a bridge, and a great place for a doggie drink from Baiting Brook.

Without crossing the brook, turn right and away from the bridge to head farther into the woods. Networks of trails crisscross the main path here, providing nice side loops for those interested in increasing the length of the hike. When you reach a four-way intersection, turn left. After you pass a sign on your right for the Birch Trail, continue as the path heads into an open meadow, then make your way down to Eagle Pond.

Known by the locals as "the dog pond," this place can get quite busy on weekends and sunny summer days. A picnic bench and a flat open field make this an ideal place to enjoy your lunch while your dog takes a swim. From the pond, continue on a path called Moore Road through a large open field. In a few minutes you will cross another bridge over Baiting Brook and then pass though a large farm field, which is often filled with corn during the growing season.

Before reaching the southern entrance to the park, take a left on a raised grassy path. When you reach a split in the trail, take a left and head back into the woods. Soon you will reconnect with the end of the Pipeline Trail and the first bridge over the brook. Continue back, retracing your steps toward the trailhead until a trail diverges to the right and enters Baiting Brook Woods, a property owned and managed by the

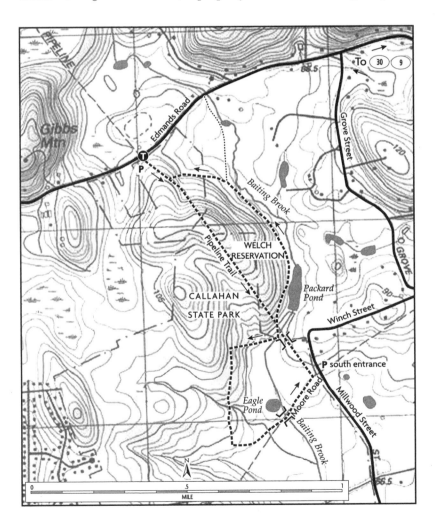

A Rhodesian Ridgeback considers a swim at Callahan State Park.

Sudbury Valley Trustees. This trail runs parallel to Baiting Brook and can sometimes be quite muddy.

While passing the alluring Packard Pond on your right, make sure to control your dog as most of the pond is private. In just over 0.25 mile, a small loop trail leads to the right and provides another access point for water. After this cutoff, take a trail that leads to the left. This will reconnect with the Pipeline Trail, where you can take a right to get back to your vehicle.

SOUTH OF BOSTON

27. Blue Hills Reservation: Great Blue Hill

Location: Milton, Canton
Distance: 2 miles round-trip
Hiking time: 1.5 hours
Elevation gain: 360 feet
Maps: Department of Conservation and Recreation; USGS Boston South; USGS Norwood
Contact: Department of Conservation and Recreation, (617) 698-1802
Pet policy: Dogs must be leashed. Dogs are not permitted on the Trailside Museum property.
Special notes: A large 19 x 27-inch four-color trail map of the Blue Hills Reservation may be purchased for $2 at the Blue Hills Park headquarters at 695 Hillside Street in Milton or at the Blue Hills Trailside Museum at 1904 Canton Avenue in Milton.

Getting there: Take Interstate 93 to exit 2B (Route 138 north). Follow the exit ramp to the first set of traffic lights. Go straight through the lights. The parking lot is 0.5 mile ahead on the right.

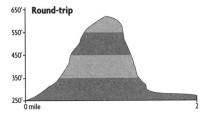

While sailing along the Atlantic coastline, early European explorers named these hills for their bluish hue. Today, the Blue Hills Reservation stretches over 7000 acres from Quincy to Dedham, Milton to Randolph, and provides a green oasis within minutes of downtown Boston. Highest

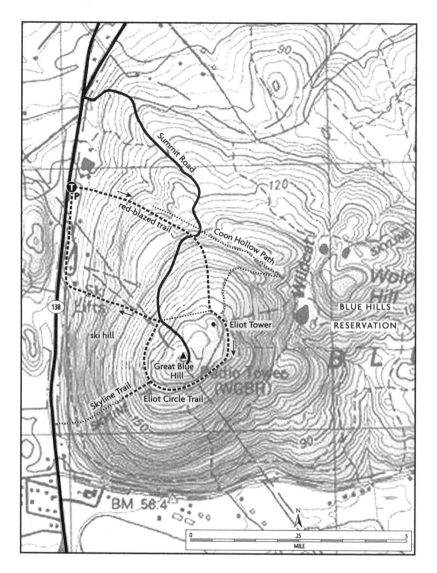

of the twenty-two hills in the chain, Great Blue Hill rises 635 feet above the surrounding towns. With its varied terrain, scenic vistas, and 125 miles of trails, the Blue Hills Reservation offers year-round enjoyment for you and your dog.

From the parking area, stop at the kiosk to take a look at a trail map of the reservation. Maps can also be bought inside the museum, but your pup will have to wait at the vehicle since no dogs are allowed near the buildings. This hike follows the red-blazed trail and is the quickest way to the summit of Great Blue Hill. Rocks and roots line the trail, and large wooden logs are placed into the hillside to help with the ascent. Much of the trail is well shaded, and even on a warm day the beginning of the hike is quite pleasant.

In less than twenty minutes, you will cross a paved road. The Summit Road, which is closed to vehicles, offers another pleasant option for reaching the summit. If you want to walk through the woods, cross the road and continue on the red-blazed trail. A couple of clearings along the way offer nice views to the south and west. Large pieces of bedrock are exposed along the trail. Soon you will reach the Eliot Tower, a stone structure named for Charles W. Eliot, the landscape architect and son of the former president of Harvard University who saw the tremendous need to preserve and manage land through public ownership.

For a 360-degree view, walk up the stone steps to the top of the tower. On a clear day you view the entire reservation, the Boston skyline, and the Atlantic Ocean. Multiple benches provide a great place for a picnic. A popular destination for families with children, the tower often becomes quite crowded. To avoid the crowds, continue past the tower, southwest on the blue-blazed Skyline Trail. Look for the Blue Hills

A scenic vista from the top of Eliot Tower

Weather Observatory on your right; it is a National Historic Landmark. The Skyline Trail will break off to the left on a smaller trail that leads to a large open rocky outcropping. This spot has fantastic views. It's also less visited and a good place to take a water break.

Once ready to move on, return to the main trail and turn left on Eliot Circle, which heads toward the Blue Hills Ski Area. When you reach the top of the main ski run, turn left and follow a winding trail down the slope. At the bottom of the hill you will reach a small ski lodge. Turn right onto a paved road and follow it down the hill and back to the parking area.

Alternative: If you plan to loop back while the ski slope is open, pick up the red-blazed Coon Hollow Path from Eliot Tower. This trail heads north and then gently descends back down to the Trailside Museum parking area.

28. Blue Hills Reservation: Ponkapoag Pond

Location: Canton
Distance: 4 miles round-trip
Hiking time: 2 hours
Elevation gain: Negligible
Maps: Department of Conservation and Recreation; USGS Norwood
Contact: Department of Conservation and Recreation, (617) 698-1802
Pet policy: Dogs must be leashed.
Special notes: A large 19 x 27-inch four-color trail map of the Blue Hills Reservation may be purchased for $2 at the Blue Hills Park Headquarters at 695 Hillside Street in Milton or at the Blue Hills Trailside Museum at 1904 Canton Avenue in Milton.

Getting there: Take Interstate 93 south to exit 2A (Route 138 south). Travel for 0.5 mile, and turn left into the Ponkapoag Golf Course parking area. Park at the far end of the lot near a wooden kiosk.

At 230 acres, Ponkapoag Pond is the largest and most remote body of water found within the Blue Hills Reservation. This walk on one of the less commonly traveled trails will provide you and your pup with peace and relaxation, all within a short drive from the hustle and bustle of the city. Visit during fall to enjoy the beautiful autumn colors reflected on the lake.

Ponkapoag Pond with Great Blue Hill in the distance

From the parking lot, stop at the kiosk to examine a good map of the reservation. Continue to the right of the buildings on a paved road lined with large maple trees. Fittingly named the "Avenue of Maples," this road is not open to traffic, but watch out for an occasional golf cart. At the end of the road, turn right and walk through a gate onto a smooth dirt path. Green disks mark this trail as it travels around the circumference of the pond.

The path is well shaded and even on a warm day you'll remain comfortable. Access to the water is plentiful, as multiple side trails bring you down to the water's edge. In 0.8 mile you will reach a small parking area where boaters access the water from a small beach. Fishermans Beach offers stunning views of the pond and Great Blue Hill. Your pup will enjoy taking a dip in the clear, cool water.

Continuing east, and then north along a wider dirt road, the trail passes the Appalachian Mountain Club's (AMC) Ponkapoag Camp. Twenty cabins dot the landscape but are well hidden within the woods. Stay to the right of the cabins, walking through a day-use parking area to follow the trail.

The trail becomes narrower as it ascends a small bluff overlooking the pond. The trail then joins another dirt road that leads down to a YMCA camp. During summer, this road is more heavily used, so be mindful of

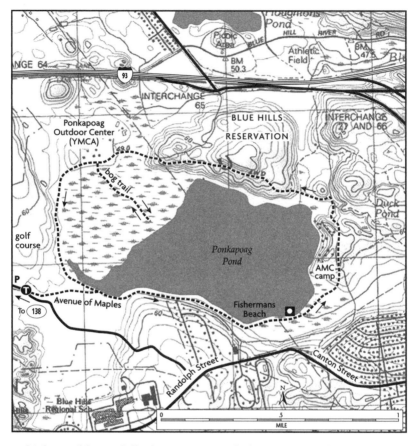

vehicles and buses full of campers. Just before reaching the camp, turn left and pass through a parking area on a trail that leads to a large stone marker and an educational kiosk. To the left is a 0.5-mile trail that leads into the Ponkapoag bog, which is an Atlantic white cedar bog. The trail is lined with red oaks and white pines on the shoreline, followed by Atlantic white cedars and blueberry bushes. The trail then clears, and ends in the open water of the pond. Boardwalks line this trail, but if you choose to take this side trip, be prepared to get wet.

After passing the bog, walk though another gate, as the trail proceeds back toward the golf course. When you reach a clearing, a small section of the trail goes directly through part of the course. Yield to any golfers at play, and continue to skirt the edge of the course, once again on a wooded trail that will take you to the Avenue of Maples, where you turn right to get back to your vehicle.

29. Wilson Mountain Reservation

Location: Dedham
Distance: 2 miles loop
Hiking time: 1.5 hours
Elevation gain: Negligible
Maps: Department of Conservation and Recreation; USGS Norwood
Contact: Department of Conservation and Recreation, (617) 333-7404
Pet policy: Dogs must be leashed.

Getting there: From Interstate 95, take exit 17 onto Route 135, heading east toward Dedham. The parking lot is 0.5 mile down the road, just before the playing fields on the right.

With over 200 wooded acres, Wilson Mountain Reservation's shaded trails, rocky outcroppings, and streams make it an ideal place to bring your dog for a hike. Protected in the mid-1990s from development, this reservation is one of the largest open spaces in the town of Dedham. The Department of Conservation and Recreation has marked two loop trails here. The 0.75-mile red-blazed loop circles Wilson Mountain in the northeast section of the property. The 2-mile green-blazed loop meanders along a stream and through a swamp before joining the red-blazed trail back to the reservation entrance. This hike is a combination of the two trails.

From the parking area, take a look at the kiosk, which displays a good map of the property. Heavy poison ivy grows near the trailhead,

Razzy is ready for a water break at Wilson Mountain.

so remember "Leaves of three, let it be!" Take the green-blazed trail to the right into the woods. Soon you will cross a small stream, the first of many crossings on this first section of trail. Water levels vary depending on the time of year, so bring water for you and the pooch. The trail continues, passing large boulders and rocky outcroppings. A section of the trail runs parallel to Route 135, so have good control over your dog.

Heading south, continue to follow the green disks as the trail travels adjacent to the swamp. Turning left, the trail crosses the swamp on a series of wooden boards. When you reach the next intersection, turn right and slowly ascend the hillside through a grove of mountain laurels. Visit in spring to enjoy the flowers in bloom. Passing a trail that veers back to the

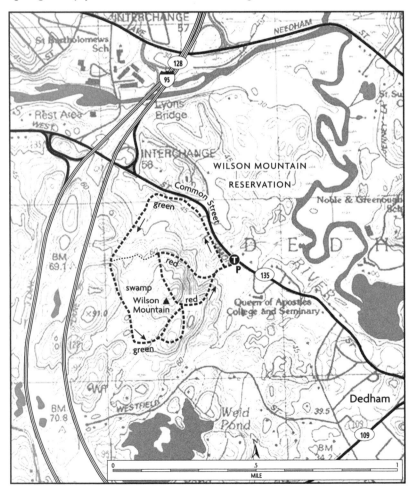

left, continue to the right until you reach the intersection of the red and green trails. For the short route back to your vehicle, head to the right as the red and green trails lead back to the parking area.

If you choose to continue, turn left and head up the slope on the red-blazed trail, which passes a series of interesting rock formations on the right. Soon you will reach a large boulder and a small clearing: a nice place to eat a snack. (**Note:** Watch out for stray pieces of broken glass at this popular picnic spot.) The trail continues, descending down the hill. (Ignore a side trail that heads left.) The trail then makes a sharp right-hand turn, continuing downward through the mixed woodland of maple, oak, hemlock, and birch. Pass another trail on the left and continue straight ahead to the parking area.

30. Rocky Woods

Location: Medfield
Distance: 3–3.5 miles round-trip
Hiking time: 1.5 to 2 hours
Elevation gain: Negligible, 170 feet to the top of Cedar Hill
Maps: The Trustees of Reservations; USGS Medfield
Contact: The Trustees of Reservations, (781) 784-0567
Pet policy: Dog walking at Rocky Woods is subject to a Green Dogs permit. No dogs are allowed on Sunday afternoons from noon to closing. Chickering Pond is off limits to dogs.
Special notes: Admission for Trustees members is free. Nonmembers: adult $3, child (12 and under) free. Fees collected by ranger on weekends and holidays; honor system applies all other times.

Getting there: From Interstate 95, take exit 16B and follow Route 109 west for 5.7 miles through Westwood and into Medfield. Turn right (hairpin turn) in Medfield onto Hartford Street and follow it for 0.6 mile to the entrance and parking area on the left.

With 491 acres to explore, Rocky Woods is a place that definitely lives up to its name. Used in the 1700s as a woodlot and quarry, this reservation now features over six miles of footpaths through rolling hills of white pine and red oak. The area's high water table—part of both the Neponset River Watershed and the Charles River Watershed—forms wetlands throughout

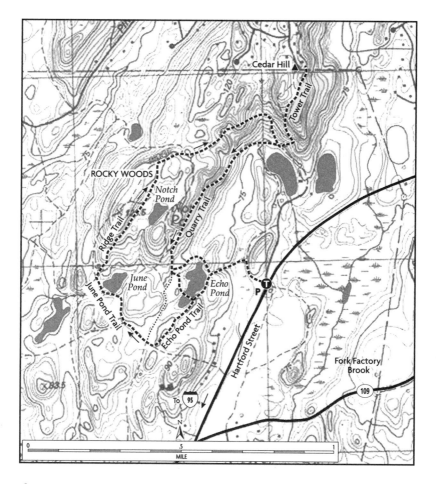

the reservation. Through the Trustees of Reservation's (TTOR) Green Dog Program, dogs are able to enjoy parts of this reservation leash free after receiving a permit. Refer to the TTOR map for updated rules and regulations for the property.

From the parking area just past the ranger station, begin your hike on the Loop Trail. Travel on this wide path until you reach a junction, where you turn slightly left onto the Echo Pond Trail. Follow this trail, keeping the pond to your right. At the next intersection, take a right onto the June Pond Trail. Watch for June Pond (which may be dry in summer), and at marker 12 turn right onto the Ridge Trail.

Opposite: A light dusting of snow covers the trail in Rocky Woods.

The Ridge Trail reminds you why early settlers called this magical place Rocky Woods, as you pass tall stands of beech and birch and a smattering of large boulders. When you reach marker 7 and the intersection with the Harwood Notch Trail, continue on the Ridge Trail. When you reach marker 4, you have a choice: (1) take a 30-minute detour and climb along the Tower Trail to the top of Cedar Hill, where the views are well worth the small detour, or (2) continue to the right along the Quarry Trail.

Once on the easy-on-the-paws Quarry Trail, walk for 0.5 mile until you reach marker 6, and turn left on the Hardwood Notch Trail. As you continue, look to the left for a small path that leads to Echo Pond. If you want to continue leash free around the pond, go toward the left; otherwise leash up and cross over the small footbridge. Both paths reconnect with the Echo Pond Trail and the Loop Trail, which bring you back to the parking area.

31. Noon Hill

Location: Medfield
Distance: 2.5 miles
Hiking time: 1 hour
Elevation gain: 240 feet
Maps: The Trustees of Reservations; USGS Medfield
Contact: The Trustees of Reservations, (781) 784-0567
Pet policy: Dogs are allowed on leash or under voice control.
Special notes: Adjacent to Noon Hill is a gun club. If your dog
spooks easily, bring a leash.

Getting there: From the intersection of Routes 27 and 109 in Medfield, take Route 109 west for 0.1 mile and immediately turn left onto Causeway Street and follow it for 1.3 miles. Turn left onto Noon Hill Street. The

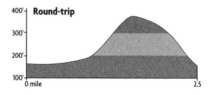

entrance and a small parking area are 0.2 mile up on the right.

With 4.5 miles of leash-free trails, one can spend an entire morning exploring Noon Hill (204 acres) and the adjacent Henry L. Shattuck

A happy hiker

Reservation, which includes an additional 225 acres along the Charles River. At 370 feet, Noon Hill rises gently above the surrounding landscape, offering extensive views south across the undulating hills of Walpole and Norfolk. Depressions found in the hillsides remind us of our glacial past. Noon Hill's thickly wooded slopes are forested with hemlock, pine, beech, and birch.

From the parking area, begin on a mostly flat trail lined on both sides with stone walls. The large pine trees provide much-needed shade in summer. When you reach a fork in the path, continue straight until the paths diverge again. At marker 4, stay to the left and follow the trail that climbs steadily to the top of Noon Hill. Once you have reached the top, the trail flattens and continues along the ridgeline. When you reach marker 7, turn left to reach a scenic overlook. Take a picnic lunch to this spot, and as midday sun passes over the ridge of Noon Hill, you will know why the reservation received its name.

Once you have returned to the trail, continue the loop in a clockwise direction. Continue along until you reach the main trail that leads back to where you started. When you reach marker 1, turn left and take a quick loop around Holt Pond. This mill pond was created in 1764 when Sawmill Brook was dammed. If you return to your vehicle and your pup is still full of energy, travel across Causeway Street to enter Shattuck Reservation. Shattuck Reservation's diverse landscapes, with 1.5 miles of trail, include a forested upland filled with oak and pine overlooking a meadow and a red maple swamp.

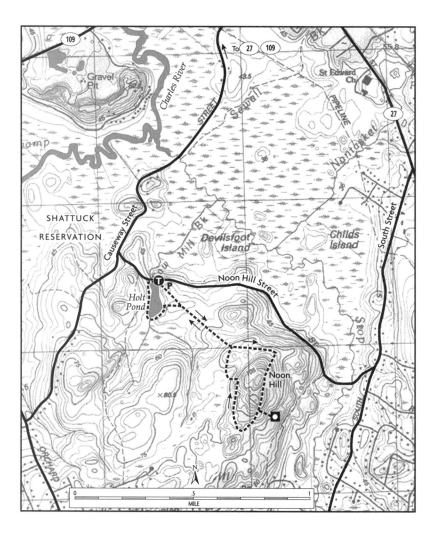

32. Whitney and Thayer Woods

Location: Cohasset and Hingham
Distance: 2.5 miles round-trip
Hiking time: 2 hours
Elevation gain: 130 feet
Maps: The Trustees of Reservations; USGS Cohasset
Contact: The Trustees of Reservations, (781) 740-7233
Pet policy: Dogs must be under voice control or kept on a leash at all times.
Special notes: Many of these trails cross onto private land. Please be respectful by staying on the trail.

Getting there: From Route 3, take exit 14 and follow Route 228 north for 6.5 miles through Hingham. Turn right onto Route 3A east and follow it for 2 miles to the entrance and parking area on the right, opposite Sohier Street.

Whitney and Thayer Woods—originally the "Common Lands of the Hingham Planters"—came into existence thanks to a few generous donations to The Trustees of Reservations. Though quite large at more than 800 acres, the woods are easily navigated thanks to trail intersection markers. With ten miles of trails, the trail network offers many combinations of various lengths. Maps are generally available at the parking lot, but it is a good idea to download the map ahead of time in case they have all been taken.

From the trailhead, follow a wide gravel road that leads into the woods. (**Note:** This road is also the driveway for a private residence, so watch for vehicles.) When you reach marker 1, turn right on Boulder Lane. In 0.75 mile you will understand how this trail got its name. The 200-ton Bigelow Boulder will be on your right, honoring the author of the first volume of *The Narrative History of Cohasset*.

After crossing a small swamp, you will reach the intersection with Whitney Road. Stay to the right at the intersection and follow Whitney Road, heading northwest. When you reach marker 10, turn left on Ayers Lane. Continue to the Milliken Memorial Path. Planted in the 1920s by Arthur N. Milliken, the flowering shrubs there memorialize his late wife, Mabel Minott Milliken. Spring and early summer are the best times to enjoy this section of the woods, when the path is lined with the brilliant

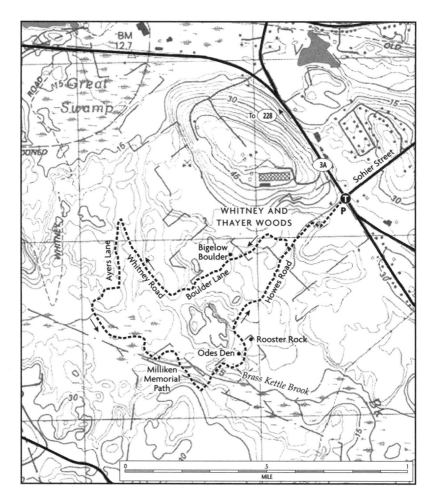

bloom of rhododendrons and azaleas. In this section of the trail, your pup will appreciate the small streams that cross the path.

At marker 20, take a smaller trail to your right toward a series of large rocky outcroppings known as Ode's Den. Apparently, the area is named after Theodore "Ode" Pritchard, who lived under one of the boulders after losing his home in 1830. After looking for Ode's old home, continue to the next intersection (marker 21) and turn right onto Howes Road. After passing Whitney Road on your left, you will reach a gate and a private property. Pass the residence on your left, and follow this gravel road for 0.5 mile back to your vehicle.

Opposite: Tasman in Ode's Den

33. Wompatuck State Park

Location: Hingham
Distance: 3.2 miles round-trip
Hiking time: 1.5 to 2 hours
Elevation gain: 130 feet
Maps: Department of Conservation and Recreation; USGS Weymouth
Contact: Department of Conservation and Recreation, (781) 749-7160; Friends of Wompatuck, (781) 741-6047
Pet policy: Dogs must be leashed in developed areas. Otherwise, dogs can be under voice control. Dogs are not allowed at Mount Blue Springs.
Special notes: The campground is open from mid-April through late October. To avoid the crowds, visit in the off-season. Hunting is permitted in season. Dates are established by the Massachusetts Division of Fisheries and Wildlife. For more information, call (508) 792-7270.

Getting there: Follow Route 3 to exit 14 (Route 228). Follow Route 228 north for approximately 5 miles to the intersection with Free Street on the right. Turn right onto Free Street and follow it 1 mile to the park entrance on the right. After stopping at the entrance to pick up a map, continue just over 0.5 mile to the third gate on the right. Pull off the road, and park on the gravel.

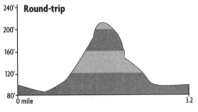

Located just 35 minutes from downtown Boston, Wompatuck State Park has a long and rich history. Originally home to Chief Josiah Wompatuck and his people, the land was deeded by the chief to English settlers in 1665. During World War II and the Korean War, the land was used as an ammunitions depot for the United States military. Today, the 3526-acre park provides opportunities for hiking, camping, biking, horseback riding, and cross-country skiing. Unlike many other state parks, "Wompy" allows well-behaved dogs to explore the trails leash free. The mostly flat land divided by a number of abandoned paved roads and hiking trails offers a plethora of places to explore with your dog.

From your vehicle, pass through the gate, and walk on the wide, paved road. Your dog can walk leash free on this closed-to-traffic road, but keep an eye out for bicyclists. Continue west, and within 0.5 mile turn left on a wooded path just before another gate—if you reach South Pleasant Street, you have walked too far. After passing a trail on your left, continue until the trail comes to a V, where you will go left. Heading south, the mostly level trail continues until reaching the edge of the campgrounds. Walk to the right on the campground's perimeter road, and rejoin the trail as it heads right back into the woods. The trail now skirts the southern edge of the campground. Want to explore the trails

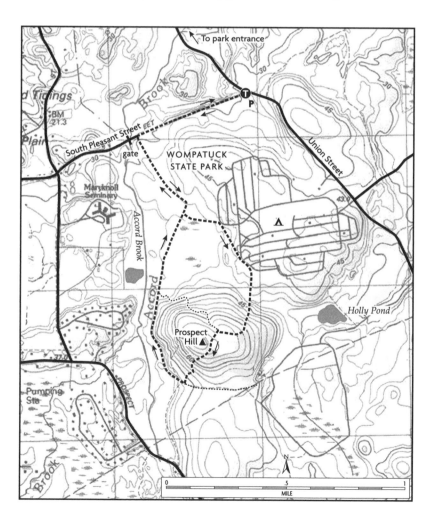

Wooden footbridges cross wet terrain in Wompatuck State Park.

over a couple of days? Call ahead and make reservations to stay at this dog-friendly campground.

At the S6 trail marker, the trail climbs steadily to the top of Prospect Hill, which is also the highest point in Hingham. A shaded summit offers a great place to have a picnic lunch. From the top, turn left, and then right on a trail with switchbacks leading downhill to the western edge of the park. A couple of different trails head down this side of the hill, but they all terminate along the same trail. At trail junction S1, turn right on a trail that runs parallel to Accord Brook. Pass some wetlands, with boardwalks lining any wet parts of the trail.

At trail marker W3, continue straight on the same trail that you used to enter the woods. Retrace your steps to the paved road and turn right, heading back to your vehicle.

34. Worlds End Reservation

Location: Hingham
Distance: 3–4.5 miles loop
Hiking time: 2 to 3 hours
Elevation gain: 120 feet
Maps: The Trustees of Reservations; USGS Weymouth
Contact: The Trustees of Reservations, (781) 740-6665
Pet policy: Dogs must be kept on a leash at all times.
Special notes: Admission for Trustees members is free. Nonmembers: adult $5.00, child (12 and under) free. Horses are permitted at this property.

Getting there: From Route 3, take exit 14 and follow Route 228 north toward Hingham for 6.5 miles. Turn left onto Route 3A and follow it for 0.4 mile. Turn right onto Summer Street and, at a major intersection with Rockland Street, continue straight. When the street becomes Martins Lane, follow it for 0.7 mile until it reaches a dead end at the entrance and parking area.

With over 4.5 miles of rolling trails and carriage paths, and a spectacular view of the Weir River, Hingham Harbor, and the Boston skyline, Worlds End is a place that you and your pup will want to go back to again and again. The 251-acre reservation is comprised of four coastal drumlins formed from deposits of receding glaciers—Pine Hill, Planters Hill, and the double drumlins of Worlds End proper. You and your dog can hike through a variety of terrains: woods, open fields, or rocky shoreline. Worlds End is a popular spot for dogs and humans alike, so visit early in the morning or on weekdays to avoid the crowds.

From the ranger station, take the trail to the left, as it climbs gently to the top of Pine Hill. As the path splits in two, go to the right and make your

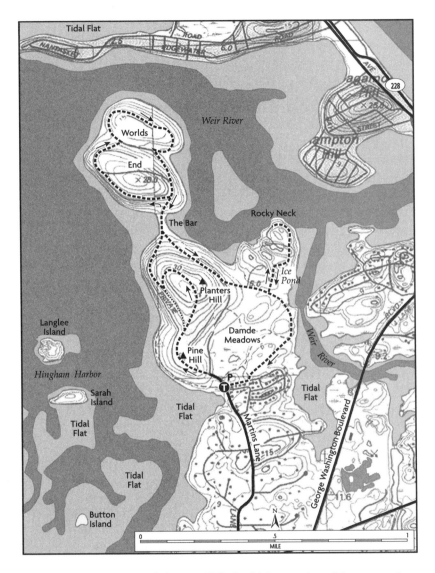

way steadily to the top of Planters Hill, the highest point of the reservation at 120 feet. Along the way, take short breaks to enjoy the amazing views.

At the bottom of the hill, you will come upon a sandbar that separates the Worlds End drumlin from Planters Hill. Early inhabitants built this area, which is now called "the bar," so they could travel freely between the two drumlins during high tide. Your pooch has a great opportunity here to splash in either the Weir River or Hingham Harbor. For those wanting to take it easy, the rocky beach to the left is fun to explore.

Once across the bar, take the trail to the left and follow it in a large circle around the outer two drumlins. Many trails crisscross this terrain, allowing you and your pooch to hike as long or as little as you want. Once you have returned to the bar, take the trail to your left and enter a more wooded area. Reaching a junction, take the trail to the left in the direction of Rocky Neck. If your pup has more energy to expend, take the side trail that veers to the left to the end of Rocky Neck. The landscape here changes dramatically, with narrow and mostly shaded trails and rocky cliffs.

Once back to the main trail, continue in a southwesterly direction. On your right, you will see the Damde Meadows Salt Marsh Restoration Project. In colonial times, Damde Meadows was a typical, healthy New England salt marsh, fed by the tidal flow from Martins Cove and the Weir River. Originally farmed for salt meadow grass, subsequent generations drained the marsh to grow hay. In recent history, Damde Meadows consisted of a shallow, open water body surrounded by stands of nonnative common reed (*Phragmites australis*) that provided little value for wildlife. The marsh is having a comeback as a result of a restoration project completed by the Trustees and other local partners.

Passing the marsh, continue for 0.25 mile to return to your vehicle.

The Boston skyline in the distance

DOGGIE DAYTRIP: CENTRAL/ WESTERN MASSACHUSETTS

35. Mount Watatic

Location: Ashby, Ashburnham
Distance: 3.6 miles round-trip
Hiking time: 2 to 3 hours
Elevation gain: 600 feet
Map: USGS Ashburnham
Contact: Department of Conservation and Recreation, (978) 597-8802
Pet policy: Dogs are allowed leashed or under voice control.
Special notes: Seasonal hunting is allowed on parts of this property.
For more information contact the Department of Conservation and Recreation.

Getting there: From Boston, travel west on Route 2 to exit 28 (Route 31 north). Follow Route 31 to Route 12 north. Follow Route 12 to Ashburnham, turn right onto Route 101 and take it to Route 119.

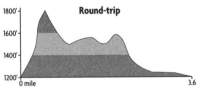

After the intersection, continue west on Route 119 for 1.4 miles. Look for a sign for Mount Watatic. The parking lot is on the right.

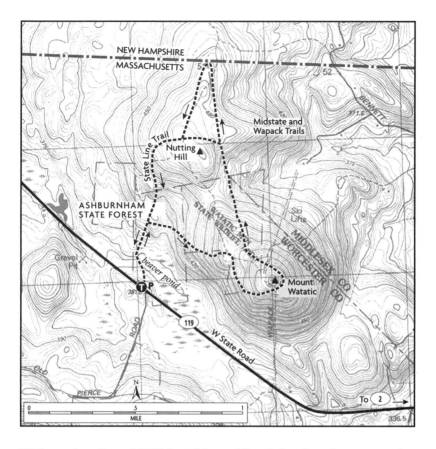

With an elevation of 1832 feet, Mount Watatic has long been a popular destination for day-trippers and through-hikers who want to experience the spectacular 360-degree views that this little mountain affords. The Mount Watatic Reservation hosts a diversity of ecological features for you and your pup to explore, including many large outcrops, steep forested slopes, wetlands, and a bald rocky summit. The Midstate Trail and Wapack Trail are two long-distance trails that traverse the reservation property.

From the parking lot follow a wide, graded path. As you proceed, you will encounter a large beaver pond on your right. A small sandy area is a great place for your pooch to take a dip on a hot summer day. In less than ten minutes, you will reach an intersection, where you will continue to the right to follow the yellow-blazed trail. Large evergreen trees provide much desired shade as you begin to ascend the mountain.

This section of trail marks the beginning of the 21-mile-long Wapack Trail. Established in 1923, the Wapack is one of the oldest interstate trails in the Northeast. Following a skyline route along the summits of Watatic, Pratt, New Ipswich, Barrett, and Temple Mountains, the trail ascends the Pack Monadnocks and ends in Greenfield, New Hampshire. In the Mount Watatic Reservation, the Wapack Trail and the Midstate Trail follow the same route. The Midstate, the younger trail of

Stopping for a rest at the top of Mount Watatic

the two, is currently 92 miles long and extends from Rhode Island to the New Hampshire border. If for any reason your dog is not tired after this hike, just pick a direction and start walking.

As you continue, the trail climbs steadily, getting steep at some points. Within about an hour, the trees begin to thin and large pieces of bedrock become exposed. It is then that you know you are nearing the top.

Once you reach the summit of Mount Watatic, pour your pooch some water, give her a good pat for the hard work, and admire the views. On a clear day, you will be able to see the Boston skyline to the southeast, Wachusett Mountain to the south, and Mount Monadnock to the northwest. Also at the summit, you will find an engraved boulder that tells the story of the conservation effort taken to protect the mountain in 2002. If the summit is busy, continue on a side trail that leads you farther to an additional section of exposed rock.

After a nice break, continue on the gravel road to the right of the trail that you took to the summit. From the gravel road, watch for a trail that veers to the left, following an old stone wall as you begin to descend the mountain. This trail down is much more gentle than the one up, even as you ascend and descend adjacent Nutting Hill. At the intersection just past the base of Nutting Hill, you can either continue to the right on a small loop to the New Hampshire border or turn left and follow the blue triangles (State Line Trail) back to your vehicle.

36. Wachusett Mountain State Reservation

Location: Princeton
Distance: 2.2 miles round-trip
Hiking time: 2 hours
Elevation gain: 600 feet
Maps: Department of Conservation and Recreation; USGS Sterling
Contact: Department of Conservation and Recreation, (978) 464-2987
Pet policy: Dogs must be leashed.
Special notes: Hunting is permitted in season. Contact the Department of Conservation and Recreation for additional information.

Getting there: From Route 2, take Route 140 south (exit 25), and follow it for 2 miles. Turn right onto Mile Hill Road. Follow Mile Hill Road for

0.5 mile to a split in the road. Take the left fork onto Mountain Road. Follow Mountain Road 1.25 miles to the top of the hill. The reservation entrance is on the right. The visitor center entrance and trailhead are on the left immediately after entering the reservation.

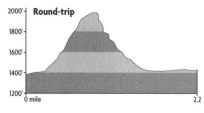

With an elevation of 2006 feet, Wachusett Mountain continues to be a popular destination in Massachusetts for hikers and their doggie companions. The nearly 3000-acre Wachusett Mountain State Reservation surrounds the summit and offers seventeen miles of trails for you and your pup to explore. On a clear day, the summit reveals views of the Boston skyline to the east, the Berkshires to the west, and Mount Monadnock to the north. The reservation's natural resources include alpine meadows, forests filled with hemlock and white birch, ponds, streams, and open fields. Before you begin, stop at the visitor center and pick up a trail map for your outing.

Panoramic views can be found at Wachusett Mountain.

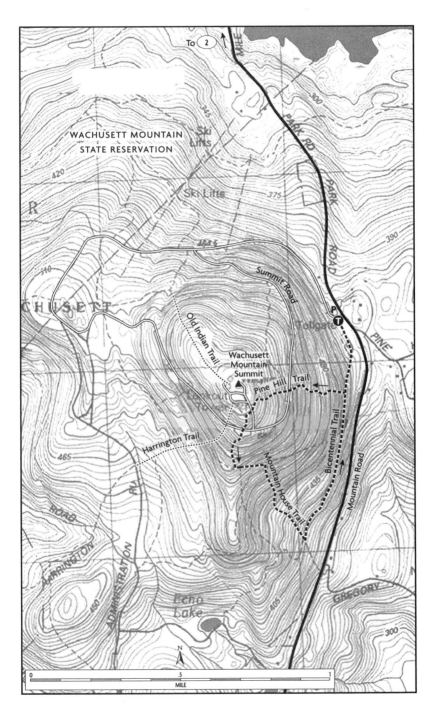

From the visitor center, head south on the Bicentennial Trail. Very soon after starting on this trail, veer to the right and join the Pine Hill Trail. This relatively short trail leads steadily to the summit and offers enjoyable views on the way up. Your dog will enjoy the terrain, with many rocks and roots to explore, but move slowly on wet days as the trail can get slippery.

As you continue up the mountain, listen closely for vehicles as you approach Summit Road, which—obviously—goes to the summit. To avoid this traffic, hike Wachusett in late fall or early spring (the road is closed in winter). If you and your dog decide to hike during hunting season, wear orange and keep your eyes out for the occasional hunter. No hunting is allowed on Sundays, so that is always a safe day to visit.

After crossing Summit Road, continue up the Pine Hill Trail to the summit. At the top, take a break and enjoy the surrounding views. A few stone platforms provide the opportunity for better vistas and a good place to have a picnic.

When you and your pooch are ready to descend, follow signs for the Mountain House Trail. As you continue down this trail, watch for local wildlife, including deer, hawks, and an occasional fox. After again crossing Summit Road, continue as the trail slopes downward. When you near Mountain Road, turn left on the Bicentennial Trail. Follow this trail for 0.75 mile back to the visitor center and your vehicle.

37. Douglas State Forest

Location: Douglas

Distance: 1–3 miles round-trip; Cedar Swamp Trail—0.7 mile round-trip; Coffee House Loop Trail—2.2 miles round-trip

Hiking time: 1.5 hours

Elevation gain: Negligible

Maps: Department of Conservation and Recreation; USGS Webster

Contact: Department of Conservation and Recreation, (508) 476-7872

Pet policy: Dogs must be leashed.

Special notes: Because this a popular recreation area in summer, visit in the off-season to avoid the crowds.

Getting there: Douglas State Forest is located on the southern border of central Massachusetts. From the Massachusetts Turnpike (Interstate 90),

A wooden footbridge crosses the Douglas State Forest cedar swamp.

take exit 10 to Route 395 south. Take exit 2 (Route 16) and go east for 5 miles. Turn right on Cedar Street, which becomes Wallum Lake Road. Go straight until you reach the main state forest entrance on the right. Continue to the parking area.

Bordering both Connecticut and Rhode Island, this popular 5730-acre state forest offers a vast network of hiking and nature trails for your dog to enjoy. The long-distance Midstate Trail runs through the forest and extends to Mount Watatic in the northern section of the state. Douglas State Forest also includes a rare Atlantic white cedar swamp, which is accessible via a boardwalk trail.

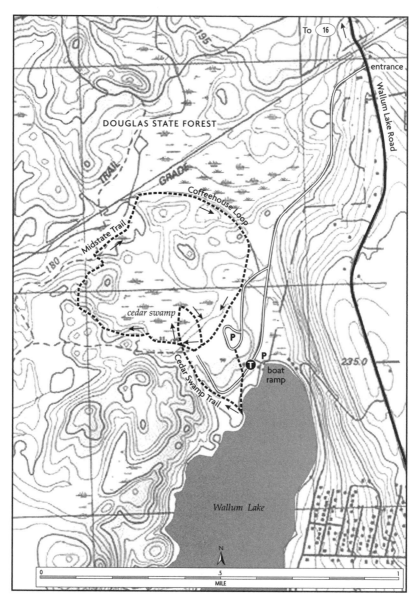

From the parking area, walk down to Wallum Lake, where you will begin your hike on the Cedar Swamp Trail. Passing a nature center on your right, the trail veers to the left and up through an evergreen grove scattered with granite boulders. When the trail intersects the Coffeehouse Loop, continue straight onto the wooden boardwalk and enter the swamp. This interesting and somewhat eerie trail winds through the trees, and the damp cool air provides a respite for your pooch. Ferns and mossy mounds cover the swamp floor.

After emerging from the cedar swamp, turn left and walk through a small quarry to return to your vehicle. If your energetic pup wants to continue, you can turn right and follow the Coffeehouse Loop Trail for an additional 2.2 miles. A section of the Coffeehouse Trail merges with the Midstate Trail, but the Midstate departs to the north as you stay on the Coffeehouse Trail heading east and then south again. The narrow, winding trail will eventually bring you back to your vehicle. In the off-season, your pooch might want to take a dip in the lake before heading home.

38. Peaked Mountain

Location: Monson
Distance: Peaked Mountain, 2 miles round-trip; Lunden Pond Loop,
 1 mile round-trip
Hiking time: 1.5 to 2 hours
Elevation gain: 467 feet
Maps: The Trustees of Reservations; USGS Monson
Contact: The Trustees of Reservations, (978) 840-4446
Pet policy: Dogs must be leashed or under voice control.

Getting there: From the Massachusetts Turnpike (Interstate 90), take Route 32 south (exit 8) toward Palmer. Pass through Palmer and continue on to Monson. After crossing over the Quaboag River, continue on Route 32 for 3 miles, turn right onto High Street, and

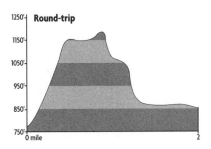

turn left immediately onto Ely Road. At the stop sign, proceed straight onto Lower Hampden Road, follow it for 2 miles, and turn left onto Butler Road. In 0.5 mile you will pass the Miller Forest Tract entrance and parking on the right, but continue for 0.7 mile to the main entrance and parking on the left.

Peaked ("pea-kid") Mountain's 1227-foot summit offers panoramic views of Mount Monadnock to the north, Wachusett Mountain to the northeast, and Connecticut's Shenipsit State Forest to the south. Now managed for timber, Peaked Mountain was once the site of a nineteenth-century charcoal operation, providing fuel for local industries. Scrub oak and deciduous hardwoods dominate this forest, which is crisscrossed with old fire roads that make this walk easy on the paws. Surrounded by the rolling New England countryside of forests, hills, and farms, this picturesque hike is a great way to spend the afternoon with your pooch.

From the trailhead, grab a map and follow the northern edge of the field onto Roslyn's Turnpike. Climbing steadily, let your dog stop at Fire Pond for a drink and frog watching. Continue, and when you reach marker 7, take a right on the West Rock Trail. At marker 10, turn right and look for marker 11, where you pick up the Valley View Trail. This

Beautiful views from the top of Peaked Mountain

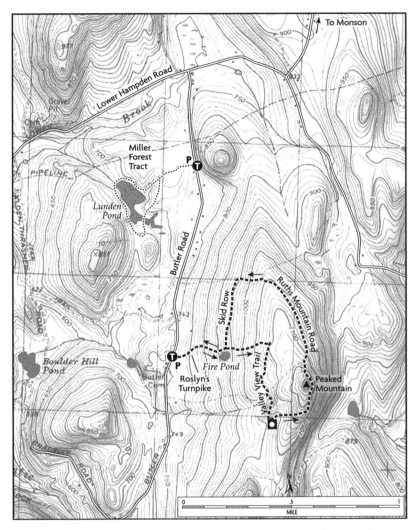

trail is properly named; as it traverses some ledges, look up and enjoy fantastic views to the south and west. Soon the trail heads north to the summit of Peaked Mountain. Stop for a picnic or enjoy the autumn colors. Before leaving the top, write your comment in the trail registry found in a peculiar mailbox attached to a tree.

Continuing away from the summit look for marker 9, passing the trail that heads left, and continue to marker 8, where you will pick up Ruths Mountain Road. This trail will lead you steadily back down the mountain. Toward the bottom of the hill, make a left onto Skid Row, an old logging road where you will find some fine old stone walls. Continue south to the end of Skid Row, and then make a right onto Roslyn's Turnpike, which will bring you back to your vehicle.

If your pup wants to swim after this climb, stop at the Miller Forest Tract on your way home. Walking along the shoreline trail that encircles Lunden Pond is a great way to end the day.

39. Mount Tom State Reservation

Location: Holyoke, Easthampton
Distance: 1.5 miles loop
Hiking time: 1 hour
Elevation gain: 270 feet
Maps: Department of Conservation and Recreation; USGS Mount Tom
Contact: Department of Conservation and Recreation, (413) 534-1186
Pet policy: Dogs must be leashed.

Getting there: From Route 91 north, take exit 17A to U.S. Highway 5 north. Travel 4 miles, and turn left on Reservation Road. Once inside the reservation, follow Smiths Ferry Road. Pick up a map at the visitor center. Continue until you see the parking area for the Beau Bridge Trail. Turn right into the lot, and drive to the left where you can park on the western edge of the lot.

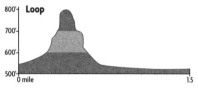

Mount Tom, one of the state's oldest reservations (established in 1903), lays claim to an unparalleled view of the Connecticut River Valley, the Berkshire Mountains, and the Pelham Hills. This 2082-acre reservation offers twenty miles of hiking and walking trails for endless hours of fun for you and your dog. In addition, Mount Tom is one of the premier hawk-watching spots in New England. Hundreds of them can be seen on a good day. Red-tailed hawk, Cooper's hawk, American kestrel, peregrine falcon, and northern harrier are some of the migrating raptors. October is fall foliage time, and the views at Mount Tom are absolutely amazing for taking in all the colors.

Two locals take a break with their dog at Mount Tom.

To begin this walk, pick up the Metacomet–Monadnock Trail (M–M Trail) where it intersects the far end of the parking area. The M–M Trail is a long-distance hiking footpath that is maintained by the Appalachian Mountain Club and other volunteers. It is approximately 114 miles from the Metacomet Trail on the Connecticut state line to Mount Monadnock in New Hampshire.

Look for the white blazes and take the M–M Trail heading north. Continue on this trail, as it climbs steadily to the top of Goat Peak (elevation 822 feet). Once you have reached the top, take a break to catch your breath at the bench that overlooks Easthampton. If you want to go a bit higher, head to the lookout tower, but you may want to leave your pup waiting at the bottom. From the top you have 360-degree views.

After soaking up the scenery, continue down along the M–M Trail as it crosses over a paved but unused road. In about 0.25 mile, turn right on the blue-blazed Beau Bridge Trail. Follow this trail as it continues down toward Cascade Brook. Once you have reached the brook, turn right as the trail proceeds back and forth across the brook on a series of footbridges. Your pup will have many opportunities to take a dip in the

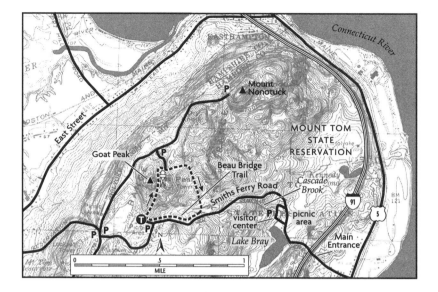

cool, clear pools on the edge of the brook. Watch your footing on the footbridges, as they become slippery when damp. Eventually, this trail will bring you back to the eastern edge of the parking area. Walk across the parking area back to your vehicle.

40. Beartown State Forest

Location: Monterey
Distance: 1.5 miles round-trip
Hiking time: 1 hour
Elevation gain: Negligible
Maps: Department of Conservation and Recreation; USGS Otis
Contact: Department of Conservation and Recreation, (413) 528-0904
Pet policy: Leashed pets are permitted, except on the beach lawn.
Special notes: A $5 fee per vehicle is charged from May through mid-October. Hunting is allowed in season, so proceed with caution. Don't forget you are in black bear country. Take appropriate precautions with food so as not to attract bears.

Getting there: From the Massachusetts Turnpike (Interstate 90), take exit 2 in Lee. Follow Route 102 west for 4.7 miles to Stockbridge. Turn left and follow Route 7 south for 6.1 miles to Great Barrington. Turn left and follow Route 23 east for 5.3 miles to Monterey. Turn left onto Blue Hill Road, then follow the brown lead-in signs for 2.2 miles to the park entrance on the right. Follow Benedict Pond Road until you reach the parking lot for Benedict Pond on the left.

With over 12,000 acres to explore, the thought of hiking in Beartown State Forest may seem overwhelming. The Benedict Pond Loop Trail is a good place to start as it offers wonderful access to the water and the

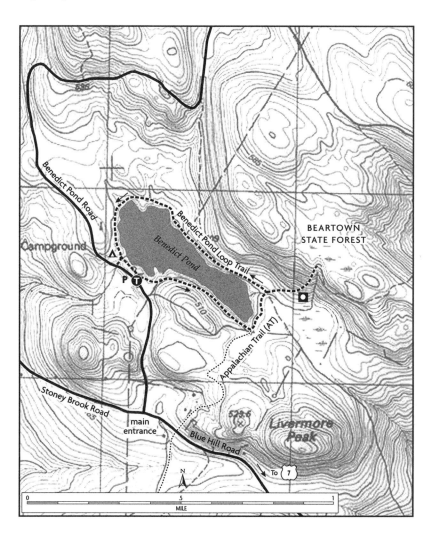

woods, and it connects to the Appalachian Trail (AT) for those who want to take a bit more of a hike. During the warm months, the pristine 35-acre pond attracts swimmers, boaters, and fishermen, but try visiting in late fall and early spring to avoid the crowds. Year-round camping is also available at Beartown, giving you and your pooch the opportunity to spend a few days exploring the trails.

From the parking area, head toward the pond and turn right on the Benedict Pond Loop Trail. This trail is relatively flat but can be rocky and filled with stumps. Wear sturdy boots, as the trail can often be wet. On the far end of the pond, the Appalachian Trail follows the Benedict Pond Loop. If you're looking for a bit more of a hike than the fairly easy Loop Trail, follow the AT north a bit, up and away from the Benedict Pond Loop Trail. In 0.5 mile, a scenic vista of the southern Berkshires appears. For a nice picnic spot, continue on the AT another mile to a backcountry lean-to.

On your way back around the Benedict Pond Loop, your dog might enjoy taking a swim. Watch for wildlife. Beartown is home to bear, deer,

The Appalachian Trail meanders through Beartown State Forest.

bobcat, and other wildlife. Beavers are known to be active in the pond, and dens can often be seen from the shore. Continue on the trail, pass the campground, cross over a small dam, and return to the parking area where you began.

41. Monument Mountain

Location: Great Barrington
Distance: 2.5 miles loop
Hiking time: 2 hours
Elevation gain: 700 feet
Maps: The Trustees of Reservations; USGS Great Barrington
Contact: The Trustees of Reservations, (413) 298-3239
Pet policy: Dogs must be leashed.
Special notes: Seasonal hunting is permitted at this property. For more information, contact The Trustees of Reservations.

Getting there: From the intersection of Routes 7 and 102 at the Red Lion Inn in Stockbridge center, take Route 7 south and follow it for 3 miles. The parking area is on the right. From Great Barrington, take Route 7 north and follow it for 4 miles to the parking on the left.

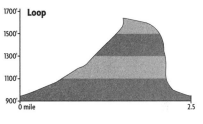

For almost two centuries, Monument Mountain has been a source of inspiration for many artists, including poets, novelists, and painters. During William Cullen Bryant's stay in Great Barrington in the early 1800s, he wrote an expressive poem entitled "Monument Mountain," which tells the story of a Mohican maiden whose forbidden love for her cousin led her to leap to her death from the mountain's cliffs. A rock cairn marks the spot where she lies buried, giving the mountain its name—Mountain of the Monument.

With more than 20,000 visitors a year—too many, by some standards—the hike to Squaw Peak is a popular annual ritual. On a beautiful fall day, the 56-spot parking lot often will be brimming with vehicles. To avoid the crowds, you and your dog should visit early in the morning or on weekdays. The summit is spectacular and offers panoramic views of southern Berkshire County. A variety of trails lead through a white pine and oak forest, and mountain laurel, hemlock, maple, and birch also dot the landscape.

Start at the parking area, grab a map at the interpretive board, and head to the right to begin your hike. This trail climbs steadily and sometimes steeply over 600 feet to Inscription Rock. Along the way, you can view a beautiful waterfall and cross over a crystal clear stream that provides your pup with a cool drink on a warm day.

Take a moment to read some history of the mountain at Inscription Rock, and then continue to the left up to Squaw Peak. The trail steepens as you and your furry friend climb a "staircase" made up of quartzite rock. Watch your footing and beware of getting tangled with the leash, as some of the trail demands sure footing. Once at the rocky summit,

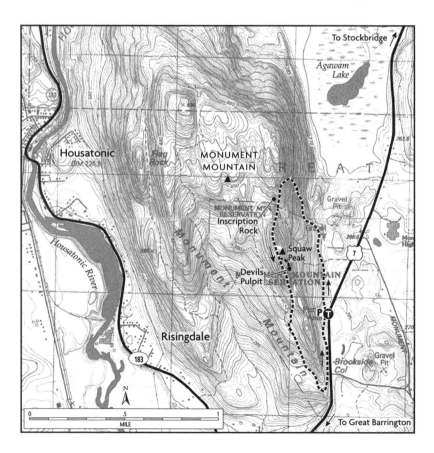

At the top of Monument Mountain

enjoy the views of Beartown State Forest to the east and the Taconic Hills to the west.

When you are done with your break, continue following the ridge until you reach a spur heading to your left. This side trail will take you to a ledge called the Devils Pulpit where you can view the pillar of stones that is the "monument" for which the mountain was named. Return to the main trail, and you'll encounter a few more viewpoints as the trail descends to an old woods road. Turn left and follow the trail back to the parking area.

42. October Mountain State Forest

Location: Lee
Distance: 3.3 miles round-trip
Hiking time: 1.5 hours
Elevation gain: Negligible
Maps: Department of Conservation and Recreation; USGS East Lee
Contact: Department of Conservation and Recreation, (413) 243-1778

Pet policy: Dogs must be leashed.

Special notes: Hunting is permitted in season, for more information contact Department of Conservation and Recreation. Don't forget you are in black bear country. Take appropriate precautions with food so as not to attract bears.

Getting there: From the Massachusetts Turnpike (Interstate 90), take exit 2 in Lee. Follow Route 20 for about 5 miles and turn left on Becket Road. Continue as this becomes Yokum Pond Road. Take a slight right at County Road, and then turn left at McNerney Road. This becomes Washington Mountain Road, which you follow for 3 miles. Turn left on West Branch Road and follow it to a four-way stop. Continue straight to parking for the Washington Mountain Marsh Trail.

October Mountain State Forest (OMSF) is the largest state forest in Massachusetts. Writer Herman Melville is attributed with naming "October Mountain," having enjoyed the spectacular fall scenery from his home

Bog bridges help the hiker navigate the Washington Mountain Marsh.

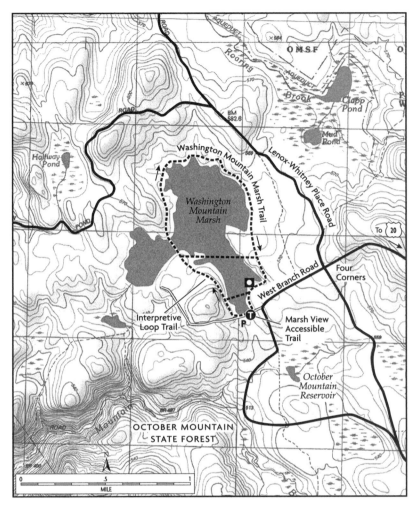

in Pittsfield. Trails, including parts of the Appalachian Trail, are available for every type of dog. With 16,500 acres—25 square miles—of area, choosing just one hike is difficult, but the Washington Mountain Marsh Trail is a nice place to start.

Often overlooked due to its location in the center of the state forest, the Washington Mountain Marsh was supposed to be a lake. A failed attempt to dam the area in the 1980s left a unique wet meadow, home to a plethora of plants and animals. A series of trails weaves through the area, offering a variety of opportunities to get up close and personal with this boggy fen.

From the parking area, follow a packed gravel trail for 0.2 mile. Along the way on your right you might notice an old cemetery and some cellar holes from the nineteenth century. When you reach an overlook, turn left and begin walking on the blue-blazed Interpretive Loop Trail. The trail descends to a series of bog bridges, where your dog might like to go for a dip, but hold tight to your leash to avoid a mucky mess. Once on the other side of the bog, pass two trails on your left, and then move through a swampy area on more bridges. Soon the Interpretive Loop Trail will veer to the right. Take a brief detour to view the marsh and the local beaver activity.

Now you will continue straight on the Outer Loop Trail. This mostly wooded path first descends and crosses another series of bog bridges near a beaver dam. Then the path moves to higher ground and follows the northern edge of the marsh. Your dog might enjoy taking a break, as the trail crosses Washington Mountain Brook. The path then turns south, and in a little over 0.5 mile you will reach the Interpretive Loop Trail. The path now climbs another hill and weaves through the woods before rejoining the Marsh View Accessible Trail, and the route back to your vehicle.

EXPLORING SEA AND SAND: THE CAPE AND THE ISLANDS

43. Beebe Woods

Location: Falmouth
Distance: 1.6 miles round-trip
Hiking time: 1 hour
Elevation gain: Negligible
Maps: Falmouth Conservation Commission; USGS Woods Hole
Contact: Falmouth Conservation Commission, (508) 495-7445
Pet policy: Dogs must be leashed. The Animal Control Officer will monitor and strictly enforce the leash law within 500 feet of the parking area.

Getting there: Heading south on Route 28 toward Falmouth, take a right on Depot Avenue. In 0.1 mile, this road becomes Highfield Drive. Continue 0.4 mile to a large parking area adjacent to the Cape Cod Conservatory. Park near the Town of Falmouth Conservation sign and the entrance to the woods.

Hosting an extensive network of walking trails that cover miles of varied terrain, Beebe Woods is a picturesque place to visit. This unique landscape was created some 15,000 to 18,000 years ago toward the end of the last ice age. Situated on top of the glacial moraine that stretches from

Woods Hole to the Cape Cod Canal, the glacier's work is evident from the kettle hole ponds and huge boulders that dot the landscape. Gifted to the town in 1976, this 388-acre estate is open to the public for walking, cross-country skiing, horseback riding, and bird-watching. Well-marked carriage trails and a pond that lies deep within the woods will make this hike one of your dog's all-time favorites.

From the parking area, take the Highfield Loop Trail into the woods. This wide dirt path heads past a trail that enters on the left, and then continues through a stone wall. Follow the trail to the left, as a series of trails diverges off to the right. Watch for a sign that directs you to the left toward the Punch Bowl, which is also known as Deep Pond. A wooden bench provides a good rest stop along the way.

After traveling through another stone wall, you will pass a trail heading left to Georges Rock, just one of the many glacial erratics found within the woods. If your pooch is a rock climber, you might want to take a detour. On the main trail, continue straight, and then bear right at the next fork to join the Punch Bowl Trail. Ascend a small hill, then head downward to reach a four-way intersection. If your dog enjoys the water, continue straight. Roots and rocks line the trail down to the water's edge.

After your dog takes a quick dip, head left, away from the pond on the Red Dot Trail. This path runs parallel to a beautiful old stone wall. After passing through a stone wall, turn left on a trail heading southeast. This

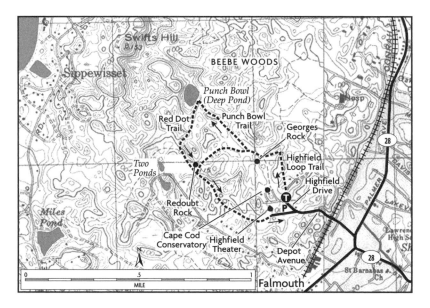

Crisscrossed paths offer a variety of options in Beebe Woods.

trail meanders through the woods and climbs steadily to reach another four-way intersection. Continue straight, descending through the forest and passing the Greengate Trail on your right. This trail ends at the High-field Theater. To return to your vehicle, take the paved path to the right that leads back to Highfield Drive. Turn left on the road, and continue straight back to the parking area.

44. Mashpee River Woodlands

Location: Mashpee
Distance: 5.2 miles round-trip
Hiking time: 2.5 hours
Elevation gain: Negligible
Maps: Mashpee Conservation Commission; USGS Cotuit
Contact: Mashpee Conservation Commission, (508) 539-1414; The Trustees of Reservations, (508) 679-2115
Pet policy: Dogs must be leashed.

The Mashpee River

Getting there: From the Route 28 rotary in Mashpee, take Route 28 south for 0.3 mile. Turn right on Quinaquissett Avenue, and continue until you reach the parking area on the right.

The Mashpee River Woodlands boasts more than eight miles of trails and wood roads through 391 acres of conservation land along the 4-mile-long Mashpee River. A mixture of fresh- and saltwater marshes, abandoned bogs, dense pine forests, and pristine shoreline make this an ideal location to take a walk with your dog. Emptying into Popponesset Bay, the Mashpee River is one of Massachusetts's finest sources of sea-run brook trout. Canoeists and anglers frequently use the river, along with birders and other wildlife enthusiasts. This hike follows the undulating contours of the woods, providing unparalleled views of each river bend below. Public access to trails exists on both sides of the river, but this hike meanders along the water's eastern shore.

From the parking area, take a quick look at the kiosk and a map of the woodlands. Taking the trail to the left, follow the sandy Long River Trail into the woods. The trail weaves through the hardwood forest and descends to the river. Rhododendrons and azaleas dot the trail, offering a splash of color in spring.

In just over 0.5 mile, a few trails diverge to the left. Stay to the right, and watch for informal trails that lead down to the river. On a warm day, the cool waters provide an oasis for a panting dog. As you continue, the trail bends away from the river, then back again, crossing over a small stream. In just less than 2 miles into the hike, you will reach Marsters Grove, a tall stand of pine trees. A wooden sign denotes the importance

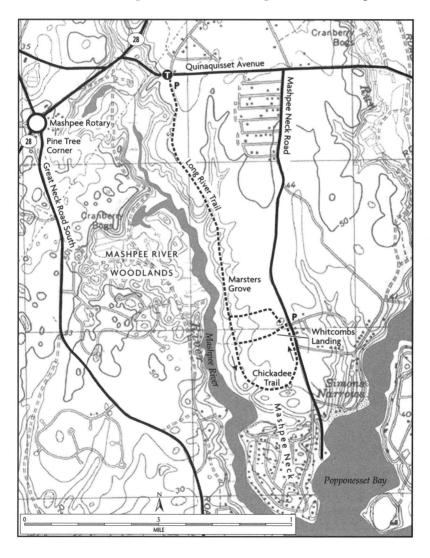

of this place, dedicated to one of the conservationists who helped protect the woodlands.

At the next intersection, continue straight on the Chickadee Trail. Follow this trail as it heads left into the woods, continuing until you reach the southern entrance to the woodlands. If you want to shorten this hike, this is where you can leave an additional vehicle off Mashpee Neck Road. From the parking area, follow a trail heading north, to where it intersects the Whitcombs Landing Trail. Turn left on this trail as it heads back down to the river. When you reach the Long River Trail, turn right to retrace your steps back to your vehicle.

45. Nickerson State Park

Location: Brewster
Distance: 3–4.5 miles round-trip
Hiking time: 2 to 3 hours
Elevation gain: Negligible
Maps: Department of Conservation and Recreation; USGS Orleans
Contact: Department of Conservation and Recreation, (508) 896-3491
Pet policy: Dogs must be leashed.
Special notes: Hiking conditions are best in the off-season to avoid the summer crowds.

Getting there: Nickerson State Park is located in southeastern Massachusetts on Cape Cod. From Boston, take Route 3 south to the Sagamore Bridge, then Route 6 to exit 12 in Orleans. Turn left off the ramp onto Route 6A west toward Brewster. Continue for about 2 miles to the park entrance on the left. Stop at the information booth to pick up a map, then continue to the boat ramp parking at the end of Flax Pond Road.

Nickerson State Park is best visited during the off-season, as it becomes quite crowded in summer with 420 campsites, miles of trails, connection to the Cape Cod Rail Trail, and eight freshwater ponds. If you decide to join the masses, you'll be happy to know that the campsites are dog friendly—just be sure to make a reservation.

The ponds in the park are known as kettle ponds and are remnants

Opposite: Cliff Pond

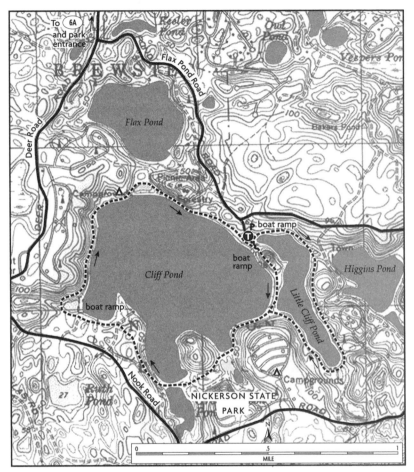

left from the last ice age when the glaciers retreated from the area. No rivers or streams feed the ponds, so water levels fluctuate from year to year based on rainfall. If the lower trail is flooded, various upland trails provide a nice alternative. This particular hike encircles Cliff Pond, the largest pond in the park.

From the parking area, follow a narrow wooded trail along the eastern edge of the pond. To the left you will be able to view Little Cliff Pond, which becomes a local ice-fishing spot in winter. The trail opens up onto a stretch of shoreline with beautiful white sand. Continue clockwise around the pond, following the shoreline until you reach a small cove and another sandy beach. Cross the beach and follow the trail that follows the flank of a steep hillside into a second larger cove.

When you reach another beach, follow a sandy trail that bisects the Cliff Pond from the adjacent large marsh on the left. The path then widens as it climbs gently, then descends back down to the pond. A network of side trails might distract you, but continue straight to keep the course. Soon the trail will reach another boat ramp. Cross the paved area and a small boardwalk to continue the trail around the rest of the pond.

Blue triangles mark the way as the trail abuts some private property adjacent to the pond. The trail climbs up a hillside into a pine forest, where you can stop for a moment to enjoy a bit of shade for your pup and a great view of the pond. After meandering gently back down to the water's edge, pass a small beach on the right, before heading back to your vehicle on the left.

If your pooch is ready for more, you can follow the small loop around Little Cliff Pond. This 1.5 miles of trail can become quite overgrown, so wear long pants and watch for poison ivy along the way. Just left of the boat ramp you will find a trail that brings you to the eastern edge of Little Cliff Pond. The trail loops clockwise around the pond until it reaches a sandy beach along Cliff Pond. From there, turn right to head back to your vehicle.

46. Trade Wind Fields Preserve

Location: Oak Bluffs, Martha's Vineyard
Distance: 1.5 miles round-trip
Hiking time: 1 to 2 hours
Elevation gain: Negligible
Maps: Martha's Vineyard Land Bank Commission; USGS Edgartown
Contact: Martha's Vineyard Land Bank Commission, (508) 627-7141
Pet policy: Dogs must be leashed or within immediate control of their owners.

Getting there: At the intersection of County, Barnes, and Wing Roads in Oak Bluffs, travel on County Road toward Edgartown for 0.5 mile. Turn left at the Land Bank sign and enter the trailhead parking area.

For Vineyard locals, Trade Wind Fields is definitely the doggie hangout. For visitors, it is a great place to bring your dog for an afternoon stroll or a morning jaunt. Many might think that taking a walk around an old airstrip sounds rather unexciting, but this classic sandplain grassland habitat and adjacent woodland provide an exceptionally beautiful place to take a hike. Watch for unusual wildflowers and grasses (bushy rockrose, purple needlegrass, sandplain blue-eyed grass, among others) that flourish in this uncommon habitat.

From the trailhead, grab a complimentary doggie waste bag and head straight onto the smoothly graded trail into the woods. Continue straight as a few smaller trails veer off on either side. Soon the trail opens up onto the airfield. Take a left there, and follow the red trail. A portion of the property continues to be used as an airstrip, so keep to the trails. If your dog can't bear the excitement of seeing a far-off dog across the field, leash up.

To follow the trail, continue on the wide dirt path that skirts the perimeter of the property. At the end of the active taxiway along Farm Neck Road, turn right and then right again, now heading in a northeasterly direction. At a junction, either stay in the fields or follow the blue trail to the left into a wooded area lined with pitch pines and eastern red cedars.

The trail becomes tree-lined as it meanders directly adjacent to a golf course. Keep your dog close by, and stay alert for stray golf balls. Continue

Dylan soaks up the scenery at Trade Wind Fields.

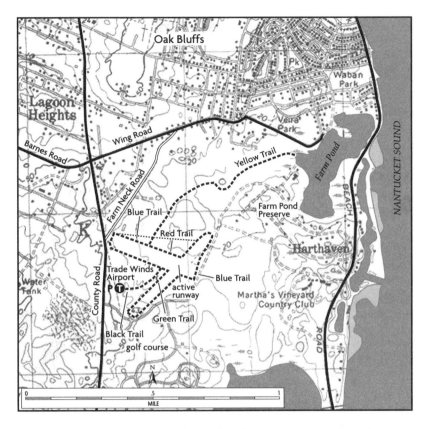

to follow the perimeter trail, then take a left into the woods and retrace your steps to the parking area.

If you want to make this hike a bit longer, you can take the trail that connects this preserve with Farm Pond Preserve. To do this, follow the blue trail and angle left on the yellow trail. Yellow markers on the trees will help you find your way. For more information on the Farm Pond Preserve, contact the Martha's Vineyard Land Bank Commission.

47. Waskosims Rock Reservation

Location: Chilmark, Martha's Vineyard
Distance: 2–3.2 miles round-trip
Hiking time: 1 to 2 hours
Elevation gain: Negligible

Maps: Martha's Vineyard Land Bank Commission, USGS Vineyard Haven

Contact: Martha's Vineyard Land Bank Commission; (508) 627-7141

Pet policy: Dogs are allowed on leash or within immediate control of their owners. Leashes required within 0.5 mile of trailhead.

Special notes: General hunting in season is allowed on this preserve, which is closed to the public during deer shotgun week. For more information, contact the Martha's Vineyard Land Bank Commission.

Getting there: From the intersection of North and State Roads in West Tisbury, travel 1.6 miles on North Road toward Chilmark. Just over the West Tisbury–Chilmark town line look for a Martha's Vineyard Land Bank sign and dirt parking area on your left.

Amounting to almost 185 acres, this reservation offers you and your canine companion a variety of terrain to explore. From the winding woodland path to the rambling meadows, you can spend an hour or an afternoon exploring the trails. The area is named for an immense glacial

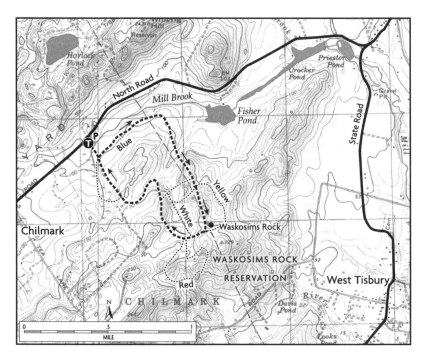

A set of stairs provides passage over an old stone wall.

boulder perched on the west end of the property. Waskosims Rock once
marked the beginning of the "Middle Line," a stone wall boundary, divid-
ing the English and Wampanoag lands in the seventeenth century.

Before hitting the trails, check out the information board at the trailhead. There you will see how the property is divided by a series of loop
trails. On a warm day, you and your pup might want to seek solitude
along the mostly shaded Blue Trail that skirts Mill Brook, but for a longer
outing make your way to the Upper Red Loop (but watch for poison ivy!).
Whatever you do, check out Waskosims Rock—it is not to be missed!

To spend a few hours at the reservation, begin at the trailhead for the
Blue Trail. Allow your pooch the opportunity to stop for a quick drink
when you cross Mill Brook. When you come to a four-way stop, take a
left and continue on the Blue Trail loop. As you and your pup continue,
test your agility skills as you cross an occasionally swampy part of the trail
on wooden planks and take some steps over a stone wall. Soon the trail
opens up to grassy fields, which are crisscrossed with multiple trails.

Follow the Blue Trail, keeping the forest to your right, until you see the Green Trail veer left into the meadow and follow it. When you reach a four-way junction with the Yellow Trail on your left, continue on the Green Trail, which makes its way up a hillside. Descending slightly, you cross paths with Waskosims Rock, a landmark along the Chilmark–West Tisbury town line.

From here you have a variety of options. If you want to continue a bit farther, take the Green Trail to the White Trail and turn left. Continue on the White Trail, which will connect you with the Upper Red Loop and take you through a densely forested area for about 0.6 mile. Another option is to take the White Trail to the right, which will direct you back to the meadow. When you see the Blue Trail on your right, continue to the left on the White Trail and then the Blue Trail. When you reach a four-way junction, continue straight and back to your vehicle.

48. Great Rock Bight Preserve

Location: Chilmark, Martha's Vineyard
Distance: 1.2 miles round-trip
Hiking time: 1 to 2 hours
Elevation gain: Negligible
Maps: Martha's Vineyard Land Bank Commission; USGS Tisbury Great Pond
Contact: Martha's Vineyard Land Bank Commission, (508) 627-7141
Pet policy: Dogs are allowed on leash or under voice control. Dogs are not allowed April 15 through June 14 due to sensitive wildlife; during summer (June 15 through Labor Day) dogs are only allowed on the beach before 10:00 AM and after 5:00 PM.
Special notes: Seasonal archery hunting is allowed on this preserve. For more information on the hunting season and regulations, contact the Martha's Vineyard Land Bank Commission.

Getting there: From the intersection of North Road and State Road in West Tisbury, travel 3.8 miles toward Chilmark on North Road. Turn right on an unimproved road at the Land Bank logo and continue to follow signs to the trailhead and parking. **Note:** The road to the trailhead is narrow and truly an unimproved roadway, so proceed with caution.

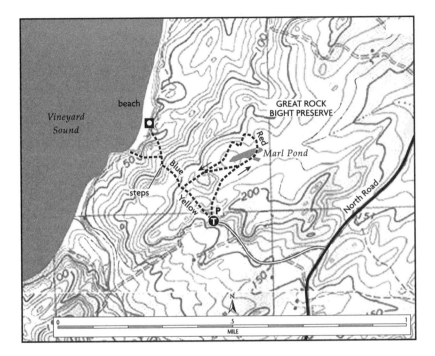

At first glance, you might think that this preserve is too far out of the way and difficult to access. You also might be put off by the many restrictions on your dog. However, if you and your pooch can time it just right, Great Rock Bight is a true gem.

Known for its parklike qualities, at just under 30 acres, Great Rock Bight's unique character derives from years of dedication from a previous property owner. The site retains a variety of magnificent trees, rolling fields, a bubbling brook, and a few small ponds. The trail descends an oceanside bluff to a sandy cove, where you can wander on Vineyard Sound along 1300 feet of beach owned by the Martha's Vineyard Land Bank.

From the trailhead, take the Blue Trail straight along a winding dirt path. Soon you will turn left, onto the Red Trail, also known as the Marl Pond Loop. This pond can get a bit swampy on the edges, but it's a good place for a quick drink. Once around the pond, this path will reconnect with the Blue Trail, where you will take a right.

Continue on the Blue Trail, and watch for a rock with a small plaque on it. This place commemorates Rebecca, an African woman once

There is access to the beach at Great Rock Bight.

enslaved on the island. After the rock, the trail turns right, narrows and begins a moderate, then steep, descent to the beach. Wooden steps help guide the way. Soon the path opens up, with great views of Vineyard Sound and the Elizabeth Islands. Take a quick break at the viewpoint before continuing down the trail to the beach. The sandy white beach is a great place to have a picnic or to let your dog take a dip. Unlike many beaches, dogs are allowed on this one in summer during morning and evening.

Two options lead back to your vehicle. The easiest way is to retrace your steps on the Blue Trail all the way back to the parking area. Another option is to start back on the Blue Trail, but turn right when you reach the Yellow Trail. The latter trail meanders though a beautiful old grove of trees before returning you to your vehicle.

49. Rodmans Hollow

Location: New Shoreham, Block Island
Distance: 2.6 miles round-trip
Hiking time: 1.5 hours
Elevation gain: Negligible
Maps: The Nature Conservancy; USGS Block Island
Contact: The Nature Conservancy, (401) 466-2129
Pet policy: Dogs must be leashed or under voice control.
Special notes: Hunting is permitted in season in some parts of Rodmans Hollow. For more information, contact The Nature Conservancy. Lyme disease is prevalent on Block Island. Wear long pants and do a thorough body check when you return home.

Getting there: Travel south from Old Harbor on Spring Street, which will become the Mohegan Trail. Take a right at "The Painted Rock" onto Lakeside Drive. At the next intersection, take a left onto Cooneymus Road. In a little over 0.5 mile, you'll come to the Rodmans Hollow sign on your left. Find parking on the right side of the road. On foot, cross the road and take the dirt path down into the hollow.

Formed over 22,000 years ago at the end of the last period of glaciation in New England, Rodmans Hollow is also known as the birthplace of conservation on Block Island. Preserved through a thirty-year partnership between the Block Island Conservancy, The Nature Conservancy, the Town of New Shoreham, and the Rhode Island Department of Environmental Management, this 230-acre property provides scenic vistas, beach access, and miles of trails for you and your pup to explore.

From the trailhead, walk down the Black Rock Trail. Follow this wide path for about 0.25 mile, where you will see on your left a wooden gate and turnstile marking the entrance to the hollow. Continue straight as the Black Rock Trail leads down to the ocean. You and your pup can access the beach via a trail down the bluff, but travel carefully as the trail is quite steep and somewhat eroded. Once down to the beach, you are free to walk in either direction, but be warned that Black Rock Beach is known to be a nude sunbathers' destination.

Back on the Black Rock Trail, retrace your steps and then turn right and continue until the trail splits. To the right is another view of the bluffs and Black Rock at low tide. Turn left and continue up the dirt road, walking through a newly protected area known as the Jones Property. This trail meanders through stands of beech, black gum, black locust, and ginkgo. Passing a trail on your left (which leads back to the Black Rock Trail) continue onward to ascend a knoll that overlooks the entire hollow and offers a wonderful panoramic vista of the ocean, clay bluffs, and surrounding farm fields.

The trail will then diverge, and if you are interested in traversing the bottom of the hollow, bear right; or bear left to keep on higher ground.

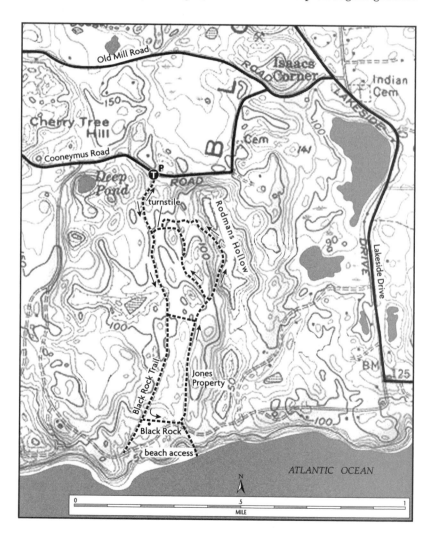

Rolling fields make for a great frolic at Rodmans Hollow.

Either way, the trails intersect, leading to the turnstile that you passed earlier in the hike. Pass through the gate, and turn right on the Black Rock Trail to retrace your way back to your vehicle.

50. Clay Head Preserve

Location: New Shoreham, Block Island
Distance: 3–4 miles round-trip
Hiking time: At least 2 hours
Elevation gain: Negligible
Maps: The Nature Conservancy; USGS Block Island
Contact: The Nature Conservancy, (401) 466-2129
Pet policy: Dogs must be leashed or under voice control.
Special notes: Between November and February, hunting is permitted during the week. Please contact The Nature Conservancy for exact rules and regulations.

Tom and Tasman get ready to explore "The Maze."

Getting there: From Old Harbor, travel up Corn Neck Road about 2.6 miles until you come to a post marker for Clay Head on the right-hand side. Turn right onto the dirt road and go straight about 0.3 mile until you reach a parking area. You will see a Clay Head interpretive sign marking the trailhead.

This spectacular hike rambles above the Atlantic Ocean along clay bluffs that offer some of the most dramatic views of any hike on Block Island. With plenty of lookout points along the way, you and your dog will enjoy feeling the mist on your face and the smell of saltwater in the air.

Heading east from the trailhead, the path meanders along, lined with large sycamore maples and a smattering of beach rose bushes on its way down to the ocean. Before reaching the beach, make a quick stop at Clay Head Swamp, where your dog might enjoy a quick drink on a hot day.

After 0.3 mile, you will reach an intersection in the trail. Turn right to visit the beach or left to continue your climb up to the clay bluffs. If you or your dog fears heights, this is a good time to leash up, as the bluffs are steep and the ocean below may look inviting to your doggie friend. The trail continues to climb steadily, then levels and stays close to the bluffs until it ends at a dirt lane. This road eventually leads to Settlers Rock and the northernmost tip of the island.

The Clay Head Trail is good for all types of people and pups, as the entire trail is scenic, and you can decide how long or short you want to make your walk. Looking for a bit more adventure? Running west of

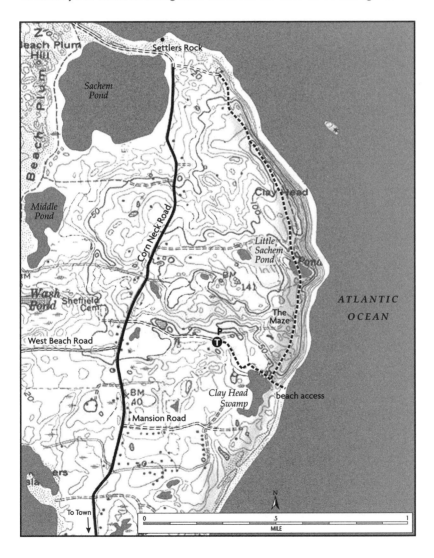

the main trail is "The Maze," a series of well-maintained but unmarked interconnecting grass trails. You can explore approximately 12 miles of trails, but proceed with caution as the trails are unmapped. Not to worry, though: if you feel like you are getting lost, just follow the sounds of the ocean, and soon you will make your way back to the main trail. When you are ready to turn back, retrace your steps to your vehicle, but don't forget to take a short frolic on the beach as dogs are allowed on Block Island beaches year-round.

CONTACT INFORMATION

The trails highlighted in this book exist today due to the hard work of many individuals and organizations protecting open space in Massachusetts. For more information on how to preserve additional land for the enjoyment of people (and dogs), contact the following groups:

National
The Nature Conservancy
205 Portland Street, Suite 400
Boston, MA 02114
(617) 227-7017
www.nature.org

The Trust for Public Land
33 Union St., 4th Floor
Boston, MA 02108
(617) 367-6200
www.tpl.org

Statewide
Massachusetts Department of
   Conservation and Recreation
251 Causeway Street
Boston, MA 02114
(617) 626-1250
www.mass.gov/dcr

New England Forestry Foundation
P.O. Box 1346
Littleton, MA 01460
(978) 952-6856
www.newenglandforestry.org

The Trustees of Reservations
Doyle Conservation Center
464 Abbott Avenue
Leominster, MA 01453
(978) 840-4446
www.thetrustees.org

Regional/Local
The Andover Village
   Improvement Society
P.O. Box 5097
Andover, MA 01810
www.avisandover.org

Appalachian Mountain Club
5 Joy Street
Boston, MA 02108
(617) 523-0636
www.outdoors.org

Boxford Trails Association/
   Boxford Open Land Trust
7 Elm Street
P.O. Box 95
Boxford, MA 01921
(978) 887-7031
www.btabolt.org

Dunstable Rural Land Trust
401 Hollis Street
Dunstable, MA 01827
www.drlt.org

Essex County Greenbelt
  Association
82 Eastern Avenue
Essex, MA 01929
(978) 768-7241
www.ecga.org

Groton Conservation Trust
P.O. Box 395
Groton, MA 01450
(978) 448-4392
www.gctrust.org

Martha's Vineyard Land Bank
  Commission
167 Main Street
Edgartown, MA 02539
(508) 627-7141
www.mvlandbank.com

Sudbury Valley Trustees
18 Wolbach Road
Sudbury, MA 01776
(978) 443-5588
www.sudburyvalleytrustees.org

ADDITIONAL RESOURCES

Books

Acker, Randy. *Field Guide: First Aid Emergency Care for the Hunting, Working, and Outdoor Dog.* Montague, MI: Wilderness Adventures Press, 1994.

Downey, JoAnna, and Christian J. Lau. *The Dog Lover's Companion to New England: The Inside Scoop on Where to Take Your Dog.* San Francisco: Avalon Travel Publishing, 2004.

Hoffman, Gary. *Hiking with Your Dog: Happy Trails—What You Really Need to Know When Taking Your Dog Hiking or Backpacking,* 3rd ed. La Crescenta, CA: Mountain N' Air Books, 2002.

Kerasote, Ted. *Merle's Door: Lessons from a Freethinking Dog.* New York: Harcourt, 2007.

Lang, Keith H., and Scott B. Comings. *On This Island: The Block Island Trail and Nature Guide.* Arlington, VA: The Nature Conservancy, 2006.

McConnell, Patricia. *The Other End of the Leash.* New York: Ballantine Books, 2003.

Mullally, Linda. *Hiking with Dogs: Becoming a Wilderness-Wise Dog Owner.* Missoula, MT: Falcon, 1999.

Pryor, Karen. *Don't Shoot the Dog: The New Art of Teaching and Training.* New York: Bantam Dell, 1999.

Smith, Charles W. G. *Massachusetts Trail Guide,* 8th ed. Boston, MA: Appalachian Mountain Club, 2004.

Dog Gear

Granite Gear (www.granitegear.com) offers a variety of backpacks, travel bowls, and leashes for your dog.

Nite Ize (www.niteize.com) makes leashes, collars, and lights that are powered by light-emitting electrodes (LEDs). Great for pet safety when traveling the trails after dark.

Olly Dog (www.ollydog.com) makes leashes and collars that are great for the trail. They are lightweight, waterproof, and totally packable. Also check out their unique travel bowls.

Planet Dog (www.planetdog.com) makes active gear for your pet, including packable bowls, leashes, and collars. Try the hands-free leash on the trail or, for an extra treat, visit the company store in Portland, Maine. A percentage of Planet Dog proceeds are donated to the Planet Dog

Foundation, whose mission is to promote and celebrate programs in which dogs serve and support their best friends.

Ruff Wear Inc. (www.ruffwear.com) offers a full line of dog accessories for the active dog. From booties to canine floatation devices, Ruff Wear can outfit your dog for any excursion.

Other Dog Necessities

Laundromutt

When your dog can't resist jumping into a swamp during your hike, head over to Laundromutt for a self-service dog-wash experience.

489 Concord Avenue
Cambridge, MA 02138
(617) 864-9274
www.laundromutt.com

Especially for Pets

Need to take an obedience class before hitting the trail? Need to buy a travel bowl or doggie booties? Especially for Pets provides one-stop shopping for dogs and their owners.

Locations: Newton, Wayland, Sudbury, Acton, Medway, and Westborough
www.especiallyforpets.com

Polka Dog Bakery

All Polka Dog creations are prepared and baked in the South End with your pup's health and heart in mind. All natural. No salt. No sugar. Visit the boutique to pick up some treats and other gear for your dog.

256 Shawmut Avenue
Boston, MA 02118
(617) 338-5155
www.polkadog.com

Gear for People

Chinook
93 Holland Street
Somerville, MA 02144
(617) 776-8616
www.chinook-davis-square.com

Eastern Mountain Sports (EMS)
Locations: Acton, Boston, Burlington, Cambridge, Canton, Hadley, Hingham, Hyannis, Lanesboro, Marlborough, Millbury, Natick, Peabody, and Plymouth
(888) 463-6367
www.ems.com

Ibex
(800) 773-9647
www.ibex.com

Isis for Women
(866) 875-8689
www.isisforwomen.com

Patagonia
346 Newbury Street
Boston, MA 02115
(617) 424-1776
www.patagonia.com

Receational Equipment Inc (REI)
Locations: Boston, Hingham, Framingham, and Reading
(800) 426-4840
www.rei.com

INDEX

ABOUT THE AUTHOR

Jenna Ringelheim grew up in Massachusetts and is in love with all things wild. An environmentalist at heart, Jenna has a bachelor's degree in environmental studies and anthropology from Skidmore College and a master's degree in urban and environmental policy and planning from Tufts University. In 2007, Jenna was selected by The Environmental Leadership Program (ELP) to be a Greater Boston Regional Fellow.

While writing this book, Jenna also worked for The Trust for Public Land, helping to protect land for people (and dogs) in Massachusetts and Rhode Island. A lifelong dog enthusiast, Jenna can often be found on the trails with her two Portuguese water dogs, Tasman and Millie.

Jenna is currently the Executive Director of Wild Gift, a leadership action organization based in Sun Valley, Idaho. This is her first book.

Jenna and Tasman enjoy the ocean breeze on Block Island.

THE MOUNTAINEERS, founded in 1906, is a nonprofit outdoor activity and conservation club, whose mission is "to explore, study, preserve, and enjoy the natural beauty of the outdoors. . . ." Based in Seattle, Washington, the club is now the third-largest such organization in the United States, with seven branches throughout Washington State.

The Mountaineers sponsors both classes and year-round outdoor activities in the Pacific Northwest, which include hiking, mountain climbing, ski-touring, snowshoeing, bicycling, camping, kayaking, nature study, sailing, and adventure travel. The club's conservation division supports environmental causes through educational activities, sponsoring legislation, and presenting informational programs.

All club activities are led by skilled, experienced instructors, who are dedicated to promoting safe and responsible enjoyment and preservation of the outdoors.

If you would like to participate in these organized outdoor activities or the club's programs, consider a membership in The Mountaineers. For information and an application, write or call The Mountaineers, Club Headquarters, 300 Third Avenue West, Seattle, WA 98119; 206-284-6310. You can also visit the club's website at www.mountaineers.org or contact The Mountaineers via email at clubmail@mountaineers.org.

The Mountaineers Books, an active, nonprofit publishing program of the club, produces guidebooks, instructional texts, historical works, natural history guides, and works on environmental conservation. All books produced by The Mountaineers Books fulfill the club's mission.

Send or call for our catalog of more than 500 outdoor titles:

The Mountaineers Books
1001 SW Klickitat Way, Suite 201
Seattle, WA 98134
800-553-4453
mbooks@mountaineersbooks.org
www.mountaineersbooks.org

The Mountaineers Books is proud to be a corporate sponsor of The Leave No Trace Center for Outdoor Ethics, whose mission is to promote and inspire responsible outdoor recreation through education, research, and partnerships. The Leave No Trace program is focused specifically on human-powered (nonmotorized) recreation.

Leave No Trace strives to educate visitors about the nature of their recreational impacts, as well as offer techniques to prevent and minimize such impacts. Leave No Trace is best understood as an educational and ethical program, not as a set of rules and regulations.

For more information, visit www.LNT.org, or call 800-332-4100.

OTHER TITLES YOU MIGHT ENJOY FROM THE MOUNTAINEERS BOOKS

Dog Park Wisdom: Real World Advice on Choosing, Caring For, and Understanding Your Canine Companion
Lisa Wogan
An entertaining guide to dog care

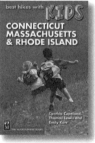

Best Hikes with Kids: Connecticut, Massachusetts, & Rhode Island
Thomas Lewis, Emily Kerr, Cynthia Copeland
Easy, accessible hikes for the whole family!

Best Hikes with Dogs: New York City and Beyond
Tammy McCarley
55 dog-friendly trails—2 hours or less from midtown Manhattan

Unleashed: Climbing Canines, Hiking Hounds, Fishing Fidos, and Other Daring Dogs
Lisa Wogan
Profiles of exuberant dogs with unimaginable skills!

Snowshoe Routes: New England
Diane Bair, Pamela Wright
75 snowshoe routes in Massachusetts, Vermont, New Hampshire, and Maine

Digital Photography Outdoors, 2nd Edition
James Martin
"A great all-in-one reference . . . You'll be well-equipped to start shooting better pictures and have a good handle on how to work smart in the field." —*Digital Photographer Magazine*